A New Church

A New Church

Not Church as Usual

Derek Jacobs

A New Church
Copyright © 2014 by Derek Jacobs. All rights reserved.

No part of this publication may be reproduced, stored in a retrieval system or transmitted in any way by any means, electronic, mechanical, photocopy, recording or otherwise without the prior permission of the author except as provided by USA copyright law.

Published By
Revival Waves of Glory Books & Publishing
PO Box 596
Litchfield, IL 62056

Revival Waves of Glory Books & Publishing is committed to excellence in the publishing industry.

Published in the United States of America

eBook: 978-1-312-58209-5
Paperback: 978-1-63443-274-0
Hardcover: 978-1-312-58208-8

REL012120 RELIGION / Christian Life / Spiritual Growth
REL108010 RELIGION / Christian Church / Growth
REL012070 RELIGION / Christian Life / Personal Growth

Table of Contents

The New Church

If you attend Church today, it may be on fire and God is moving. If we took a look at most of the Churches though we would see Church after Church barren. Churches with no fruit. This is about to change in many places because God is about to bring the hungry together.

What Causes Barrenness in Church Life?

When we talk about putting down roots or laying foundations, we often think of staying put in one place. Our God is not a camper.

The tent of meeting in the Old Testament was a simple structure designed to be easily erected and dismantled as His people followed the cloud of His presence.

The more formal structure of the temple was designed to enable people to come to grips with the same phenomena. The presence of God was enshrined in mystery within the Holy of Holies. People waited anxiously for the reemergence of the High Priest on the Day of Atonement.

The smell and spectacle of the sacrifices added to the drama of coming into the very presence of God. People were brought to that place of awe-inspiring worship as they became involved with the ongoing pageantry of the manifest presence of God in their midst.

The supernatural was commonplace. Men and women both spoke with sharpness and clarity in their representation of God.

Words were backed up with power and anointing that saved lives and brought deliverance from occult powers, famines, disasters, and human oppression.

This essence of pure relationship and raw power between God and His people has been the dominating theme of the Scriptures.

Only the form and style have changed throughout the generations—from a handmade stone altar roughly put together with materials on hand by individual men such as Abraham, Jacob, and the prophets, to the designer places of worship expressed in the tabernacle and temple.

At times these places of worship were inspired by a revelation of God's grace, mercy, and calling, such as when Jacob-in-transition to-Israel finally came to understand the desire that God had for relationship with him.

In other times and places, altars were built upon the sites of intense spiritual warfare and upon battlefields as sacrifices were offered to God on the burning embers of false gods and idol worship.

Mount Carmel and Gideon's hometown became places of cleansing and purification as the enemy was driven out and the name of the Lord revealed.

Continuity from the Old Covenant to the New was established in the person of Jesus, who became the temple of God wandering amongst a guilty and sin-ridden people.

"Destroy this temple and God will raise it up in three days," He said, referring to Himself (see Jn. 2:19). Something had happened in the hearts of the people between times.

A creeping institutionalism had given way to form without power, to style without substance, and to a performance mentality that elevated men, not God, in the presence of the people.

People did things to be seen of others; rules of behavior governed the lives of many. Leaders had become blind guides, searching the Scriptures without prophetic insight. Those who most desired the coming of the Messiah missed Him because their interpretation of Scripture was not mingled with worship, the manifest presence of God, and prophetic wisdom.

God walked among them, but they had not been trained to recognize His presence. All their teaching and distilled wisdom down through the years had left them without the faculty for discerning the glory of God.

Even when they saw signs and wonders and Jesus graciously asked them to believe in those signs as part of their journey to a wider, deeper revelation of God's presence, they could not bring themselves to part from their institutional mind-sets.

So the early Church grew up next to a hidebound institution that continued thinking that it alone held the glorious tradition of the truth of God. The old persecuted the new, which in turn eventually came against the newer works, which in time grew to be the oppressors of new moves of God till the present day.

The chronicles of the Church are littered with stories of new moves of God erupting in the earth through orthodox persecution and then settling back into conventional, narrow-minded religiosity.

Only the presence of God can prevent institutional Christianity from reducing truth to a set of rules and worship or to a meaningless time of singing without awe. Only God's presence can enable believers to confront the enemy and the evils of mankind with a powerful expression of truth combined with supernatural power.

Only God's presence is the glue that holds us all together through tensions, conflicts, and the violence of being on the front line of the battle against a depraved and intimidating foe.

We have lost the glory, the majesty, and the mystery of all that God is within Himself. The temple gave way to the synagogue and the mystery began to fade. Word stopped leading us to worship, and in time the dynamic revelation of God became a rote to live by as we waited for God to come in final deliverance.

Today's worship precedes the Word and in many places has become the platform for the teaching and the ministry of people. Our churches have lost the art of ministering to the Lord in worship and discerning the voice of the Lord in our midst (see Acts 13:1-2).

People went to the temple to participate in the mystery and the majesty of God. They went for three main reasons: to worship, to make an offering, and to pray. In the synagogue they went to hear the word of God (i.e., for teaching), to get their needs met, and to have fellowship. In the temple, the instruction and communication of God's word always led them into an experience *with* God.

In the synagogue, it often led them into debate and discussion *about* God. Meetings became man-centered instead of revolving around the presence of God. Even today in many of the newer churches, if the meeting has a lot of content and activity, it is often

the worship that gets squeezed. People go to church for good teaching or fellowship.

Our society has created intense loneliness, and people are hungry for companionship. Accordingly, it is easy to justify making our meetings into a designer-style atmosphere to attract people.

I am not against this in principle. I think all our meetings should be aimed specifically at God's desire to do particular things and achieve specific objectives. I am against stereotypes that do not bring us into the creative presence of God.

We must regain the capacity to live in the manifest presence of God. The teaching of the Word must lead people into an encounter of God Himself, not just into an experience of the church.

God has always set people within the framework of tabernacle, temple, and church who would act as catalysts to cause breakthrough into the manifest presence of the Lord. When people look at us, they should see Jesus. They should observe His love in the way that we live together.

The entrance of God's Word should produce hope, faith, life, and health to every part of our being. The presence of God is life to us. When we lose His presence or, even worse, if we have never grown up with the reality of His glory, it is inevitable that we would use the Word to relegate the supernatural to a future time of glory in Heaven rather than glory now.

God sits outside of time. He has never not been full of glory. He is altogether glorious. Everything He touches carries the fragrance and the passion of His manifest presence. He is wonderful, awe-inspiring, and magnificent. Our meetings must reflect the glory of His unchanging nature.

I love to meditate on the nature and character of the Lord. For me, He has come to be the kindest person I have ever known. He is kindhearted, gracious, loving, good-natured, and benevolent. He is generous, cordial, approachable, and thoughtful.

He is slow to anger and swift to bless. He sees the good, acknowledging the treasure and the worth in people. He inspires confidence, renews our self-worth, and puts a smile on our hearts. He is captivating, beautiful, and completely lovely.

He is strong, powerful, a force to be reckoned with, a conqueror and overcomer. He is a paradox—a fierce and mighty warrior dressed as a lamb; the king of glory and a bruised reed; a son, a servant, a prophet, a priest, and a king.

The fear of Him is the beginning of wisdom, yet His laughter makes us wriggle with pleasure. He continually brings us to points of vulnerability and weakness so that His sheer joy in Himself can be our source of strength.

Our meetings very often do not reflect His nature, but ours. They focus on our needs instead of celebrating who He is in our midst. How many of our people take time out during the day to spend just a few minutes in silent worship and awe of God?

Whatever God is, He is—infinitely. It is impossible for God not to be everlasting, endless, and eternal. He is the greatest endless and eternal expression of goodness, kindness, and grace. He is everlastingly kind and merciful, eternally loving. He loves infinitely and without boundaries. There is no end to the kindness of God.

He is also totally perfect. He never does anything partway. He completes everything He starts. "He who has begun a good work in you will complete it [literally, perfect it] until the day of Jesus Christ" (Phil. 1:6). He does everything perfectly. He is infinitely good and perfectly good. He has perfect love and grace. His love is complete, wholesome, and endlessly perfect! He is always loving because He is infinite and perfect.

He is immutable. He never changes. What God was, God is and God will be. There is no shadow of turning within Him. He is unchanging. What a relief! We all have experienced the fluctuating fortunes of human relationships and been both blessed and burned. I love the ongoing continuity of God's affection for me.

He put me in the one place where I could relate to Him in all of my changeableness. He put me into Christ so that His unchanging, infinite, and perfect love could become a constant to me as I grew up in Him.

He is never indifferent. His silence is just His silence. Never mistake His silence for detachment. He is never aloof and unresponsive. His silence is often a means to draw us into meditation, which becomes the prelude to worship and the entrance of revelation that then brings change to us.

What changes us the most is the unchangeableness of God! Whenever I reflect on the unchangeable nature of God, I want to cry. His constancy and dependability always make me resolve to be like Him.

He brings peace to me by His constancy. I feel my heart settling down into Him in the turbulence of situations and events. In crises and conflicts I find myself wanting harmony and love rather than just resolution.

To agree to disagree and remain loving friends is a sure sign that God is among us and that we are in love with Him.

God is endlessly enthusiastic about people. He has a boundless, unremitting energy.

He never stops working, yet He exudes rest and peace. He rests in and through His work. I am never quite sure where my rest in Him gives way to His rest in me. (Oh, I love Him.) On the seventh day He rested from creating, but He never ceased from maintaining what He had made.

It is typical of God that man's first day of creation and life should coincide with God's rest. Our first day began with rest, and a prime part of our relationship with God is to enter His rest. One of my personal goals is to be one of the most restful, peaceful people on the planet.

Since I have discovered rest as a major part of my relationship with the Lord, my output has increased significantly. Rest maintains worship, adoration, and focus. It promotes a God-consciousness by the Holy Spirit that increases productivity without detracting from fellowship.

The more we rest, the more we get done. Time spent resting brings us into a place where God can do in seconds what we could not do in hours under the anointing.

The more we rest, the greater the power to break through. The greater the rest, the more God prepares things around us by His hand. His wisdom increases as we sit and relax in His presence.

Our spiritual house is built on the rock of what God is really like!

To rest in the finished work of Calvary is a wonderful privilege. Lack of the presence of God is a major cause of barrenness.

Called to Be Church

I'm not sure where the Church got off track but overall it sure has. Jesus never intended for Christianity to become a religious sect. He did however want His followers to follow His footsteps in how He lived life, as designed by God, on this earth. Watching what His Father does and hearing what His Father says is what He does. That's how He's obedient to His Father's will. It's not a matter of rules or of even choosing between right and wrong but of just being obedient to His Father. In like manner, the same Father calls us. He wants us, as His children, to each become an obey-er, just like Jesus.

Being church is living Christianity 24 hours a day, seven days a week. And every child of God can do just that because the Holy Spirit is not just here to stay in a believer's life on Wednesday nights and Sunday mornings but every minute of the day, even if one is just sitting down or lying in bed. We are the temple of God, and wherever we go, we stay the same-the church of Jesus Christ.

Being church is neither going to church nor doing church activities. It is not a full-time or part-time Christian, and most of all; it is not a Sunday-going believer. It is not defining worship as attending worship services in church buildings. Also, it is not having a specialized ministry (a person who specializes in specific ministry in the church or someone who is a part of an elite group that does a specific task in the church or outside the church but is overseen by someone higher in authority like a pastor).

Wherever I go, I meet tens if not hundreds of Christians who don't care about going to church anymore. It's not that they have lost their faith, but rather that they have kept it until now. And they're afraid of losing it if they were to join a church! Most of these folks are not just pew sitters but have ministries in their local churches. Amazingly, I've also learned some have backslidden not because they were made to stumble by someone outside church, but by someone inside it!

Millions of Christians around the world are aware of this kind of Christian Modernization. They are not ignorant anymore of the two-faced mask of hypocrisy and its effect on divisions in the body.

Are these people looking for a different kind of Christianity? Are they tired of being religious? Could it be attending church -- Sunday after Sunday, week after week, month after month, and year after year, both now and forever, amen -- doesn't make you a good Christian? Otherwise, you might end up as just another brand of Christianity on the sidewalk.

"There's a lot of interest in early Christian diversity because people who have left church, and some who are still in it, are looking for another way of being a Christian." - Marcus Borg

If you really want to check on Jesus life and ministry in the gospels you will find out Jesus never did the same thing twice in the same way. In other words, He wasn't into techniques but was unpredictable. In our human strength (or perhaps more accurately weaknesses), we try to systematize everything Jesus did. For example, Peter who, after seeing heavenly glory, wanted to build Tabernacles in the mountain where Jesus was transfigured. And not only one, but three!

There's also the time when Jesus spat on the ground and made clay and put it on a blind man's eyes and commanded him to wash it in the pool. May I ask those who have a Healing of the Blind Ministry, did Jesus use a clockwise or a counterclockwise motion? Or maybe I will specialize with a Spitting Ministry. Do you want me to spit on you?

Jesus' life was never structured; He simply obeyed His Father. Singing for 30 minutes may not be worship at all. Worship is obedience to what He called us to be. That is the highest form of worship. It is the expression of our redeemed lives, our way of life. We cannot just put our Lord or His ways into a system.

Churches today are like spiritual machines. Programs are their survival kits. People love to pour their money into the machine to keep it running. But in reality, church life is like a wind: you don't know where it goes. It is a journey, a daily journey. It cannot be sewn up in the intellect; it must be uncovered during the journey.

Have you wondered why we are to be led by and walk in the Spirit? Because a disciple is a follower, a follower of Jesus' footsteps, we are on a journey. No wonder the measurement of our maturity is to be like Christ and the end of it is when we see Him face to face (1 John 3:2). So it's not joining Discipleship Class 101 or working our way through a curriculum but it is a lifelong day-to-day commitment. A "take up your cross daily and follow Me" subject. The fruit of the Spirit are not there as proof of maturity but is part of the progress of your journey toward Christ. It is not the sign of your qualification as a mature person but a quality of the life you live before everybody. It is not the end of your journey; it is your endless journey until you meet met Him.

We are not only not religious, but we're not legalists either. We are not guided by rules, but we are guarded by our freedom in Christ. Paul rightly claimed,

"Everything is permissible to me but not everything is beneficial." What a freedom we have in Christ!

Jesus was the most spiritual person on earth and He was also the most natural person on earth. Our religious assumption is that we're trying to separate our natural life from our spiritual life. When we have devotions, we think we are more holy and closer to God. We feel spiritual. But how about afterwards? When we "minister" we feel spiritual. But when we're done ministering what are we?

The only valid answer is: You are religious, not spiritual -- making Sunday a holy day just because you've gone to church, then considering Monday through Saturday unholy because you go to work. You are separating the sacred from the secular. You are not righteous, you are religious! And the danger of being religious is that it prevents you from obtaining the real thing.

The best word we have for this is "hypocrite." One man entered a church on Sunday morning and wondered why the people there ignored and avoided him. "Ah, I see," he realized. "They don't like smoking. Church people don't like smoking." So he threw away his cigarette butts. People started to welcome him, believing he was touched by God's presence in church. After church he went home, opened the cabinet and lit a piece of cigar. Next Sunday members thought he stopped smoking because of a touch from God's presence. No. It was their legalism and their religiosity. What did this man learn? He learned to play the game of hypocrisy. Where? In the church. And often pastors are the biggest hypocrites there.

God in heaven transferred His residence from a temple building to a temple body, which is Christ's church on earth. Even from the beginning, God's original intention was to stay in a Tent, which is mobile, not in a Tabernacle, which is stable. But even then God granted David's desire, but not for long. "God became flesh and dwelt [tabernacled in Greek] among us." He wants to have a movement of people, not a monument of bricks. He wants called out ones, a community, and a nation of priests. And only God can move people into such a movement of ekklesia.

Movement of ekklesia. Who can make a difference? God's only purpose for giving His people the Laws, priests, sacrifices, the Temple and circumcision was for them to be different from all peoples of the earth. But a short time later they intermarried with other nations. The pagans' gods became their gods. They became friends with the world and developed enmity toward God. Is there any difference? Instead of these nations following them, God's people became their followers. The important thing is not that we do church differently. What counts is how we live life differently.

"The Lord simply said, "I will change the understanding and expression of Christianity in one generation." - Mike Bickle

Church in Homes

God released a prophetic Word that stated, "I the Lord am going to release Revivals in homes. The reason I am touching homes is because the Church has set a structure blockage of religion. Since the birth of Jesus' primitive church, people gathering in homes has really been more the norm than the exception in most of the world. For the first three hundred years this was clearly the most accepted modality for the gathering of the people of God. And for centuries to come, in many cultures believers without access to funds, and lacking the drive to build monuments, basically met wherever they could in some of the most convenient places to edify each other, and worship God.

It is basically in the Western World, and the nations we have influenced that house churches have become more or less the weaker option to the "real" church with its own facilities holding services each weekend. In many communities "housechurching" is still labeled as the transitional mode for the gatherings of God's people until they are finally able to rent, lease, or purchase their own facilities and "go public" as a real church.

In 310 AD when Constantine converted, he actually converted "Daily Christians" into "Sunday Christians" by declaring Sunday a holiday. He built the first Cathedral, and soon a spate of cathedral building took place in Europe which included the domination of a professional priesthood, resulting in some places with the demise of the house church movement.

Still in many denominational arenas the idea of a "smaller" group has a stigma attached to it as being something "less than." While waiting for the "big," the "growing" and the "successful church."

Over a decade ago, back in the last millennium, we began to hear the predictions that even in the Western Church, the mechanics, the mode and the many forms of the church would be changing.

Christian Schwartz, the German church-growth researcher began to suggest that we were fast moving into an era of a third Reformation. His take, was that the first Reformation took place in the sixteenth century when Martin Luther rediscovered the core of the gospel: salvation by faith, the centrality of grace and of Scripture, and would be remembered as a reformation of theology.

That a second Reformation occurred in the eighteenth century when personal intimacy with Christ was rediscovered, and that it was, according to Schwartz, a reformation of spirituality.

He then suggested that an entirely new third Reformation would accompany the third millennium. And that it would be a reformation of structure or how we actually "do" church.

To say that this means solely that we should return to smaller, more intimate home type-meetings is to miss much of this full impact of this reformation. It is most profoundly seen, I believe, as a return to the kind of meeting that potentially releases the priesthood of all believers in a given setting. Notwithstanding that I also believe that that can be best accomplished within the context of "smaller" as opposed to a "bigger" group in terms of the size and dynamics of the gathering.

But the goal is not simply getting the church out of bigger buildings and into smaller, homier ones. It is about creating an environment for a people movement. It is redefining authority that has only been defined organizationally with titles, positions and property-driven visions. It is moving the church to a more collaborative, open, sourcierarchye lifestyle. And again this shift does seem to function best in smaller organic gatherings of believers where everyone has a vital part.

In these settings we become "self-feeders" rather than living dependent on an elite group of leaders to bring us the milk of the Word. In these groups we get out of the "go-to-meeting- comfort zones," and allow God to develop our missional-adventure-with God and others.

Howard Snyder, in his classic book, "The Problem of Wineskins," suggests a most basic fact, that theologically, the church does not need temples of church buildings. Church buildings are not essential to the true nature of the church. Even God's apparent preference for the tabernacle over the temple is a sign and a New Testament reminder (Acts 15), that the tabernacle emphasizes God as dynamic not static, as mobile, as a God of surprises. And shows God's people, the church, as mobile, flexible, as pilgrims. Howard notes, "Theologically, church buildings are at best necessary or practical only as a place to meet, and at worst idolatrous." (The Problem Of Wineskins, Howard A. Snyder, Touch Publications, 1966, Houston Texas, Pages 63, 64).

Maybe, just maybe, another factor or force has been creeping up on us in today's Western, building-professional-staff-driven model. To help us make a shift to the old model of the church gathering in homes, apartments, offices, and coffee shops is possibly, simply the size of our corporate wallet.

Yes, we are now hearing of churches, even in America, who are opting for a different kind of stewardship of their time, energy and money, as they remain viable in ever-shaking times.

The article I am including in this newsletter is a story of that kind of a shift. This is not a group connected with Third Day Churches, so we are not touting our own network. The following is a simple story of what caused one church in Orange County, California, to step into a new way of "doing" church.

It really is a "new day," with a permissional wind that is blowing, freeing us to follow His leading into a more creative and possibly even more effective way.

I will let the following article and some follow-up stories speak for themselves.

There's no pulpit, no preacher, no sermon and not even an offering time. But for some 70 people, it's church.

More specifically - a house church.

Across Orange County, Calif., The Well hosts five autonomous house church gatherings. Around 15 to 20 people come together at each place prepared to share what God put on their hearts that week and to "bless each other."

The gatherings don't run on a set worship service schedule or with any specific curriculum. On one Sunday, one of The Well's house churches relocated and attendees spent that day helping with the move. That was their Sunday service.

"It's a little random because we don't know what's going to happen every week, but I like this more than preaching a sermon because when it works, you really see God doing it," said Ken Eastburn, pastor of The Well.

The Well may be one of the more unique house churches in the country. A nearly 60-year-old church, The Well was originally a traditional church called First Southern Baptist of La Habra. It drew upwards of 700 people at its peak. But as the church experienced too many changes at the pulpit with pastors coming and going, attendance dwindled to about 20.

The congregation sold their building and began meeting in a 4,000 square-foot facility that cost thousands of dollars.

"It was ridiculous to spend that much money" on a building, said Eastburn who began leading the church in 2003. "Think about the millions and billions of dollars the U.S. spends on maintenance and buildings."

The shrunken congregation began praying about what to do next.

When one of the members proposed meeting in a house, Eastburn did not favor the idea at first.

But after googling "church" and "house" and meeting pastors who have adopted the house church model, he and the rest of his congregation felt "it made sense" for them to transition into homes.

"When the lease was up, we prayed, fasted and went into homes and we never looked back," Eastburn, a 48-year-old ordained Southern Baptist pastor, said.

"It was something unexpected. I wasn't looking for it," he remarked about the 2005 move. "We fell backwards into this model and I love it."

The lead pastor clarified that the transition was not prompted by finances necessarily but rather, it was "a God thing."

The transition from a traditional church to house churches has many advantages, Eastburn lists.

Most of the offering and tithes go straight to ministry works and service projects rather than to overhead costs and staff salary. Eastburn is the only paid employee in the church.

Also, there are no passive attendees. Everyone participates and the house church has the potential for creating authentic disciples.

"You can go to a conventional church and just sit there. It's much easier to hide," the house church pastor noted. But at house churches, "you can't just sit there for too long."

"Have you heard of the 80/20 rule? We have the 100 percent rule here. Everybody's involved," he said.

That kind of involvement and commitment could scare some people off. And it has.

Over the last four years, The Well has seen people come and go. While some leave because they miss the ordered structure of a traditional church, the worship or hearing "the big" sermon, many also leave because of the effort they have to put in when attending a house church.

"This is hard work. When you come to this group, you're expected to make a little sacrifice," Eastburn said. "You got to care about each other, listen to each other" and be open to sharing.

And as people open themselves up more, what typically happens is people's sins begin to surface, the Orange County pastor noted.

"You got to deal with it, or you run," he said, adding that The Well encourages groups to work together with the person when such situations arise. "A lot of people run."

"They'd rather run and not deal with it."

Another advantage to house churches is they're open source, Eastburn pointed out.

"I've heard some bad theology from the pulpit and you can't challenge the pastor right there," he said. In house churches, attendees have the opportunity to ask questions, challenge views, and even correct theology on the spot.

"Basically, anybody can put their two cents in," he noted, and "it's easy to edit on the fly and correct right there."

Eastburn currently has little concern for heresy considering they have less than 100 people and each house church is overseen by an elder who is grounded in sound doctrine. Any time a discussion may veer the wrong way theologically, Eastburn and the elders are present to steer them in the right direction.

"We're not saying we have the final word," the pastor added, "but we say 'this is aligned with what's accepted solid Christian doctrine.'"

Since moving out of the building, The Well has kept a low profile and spread only by word of mouth. But after four years, Eastburn realized they have a unique story to tell and other churches to help as more are considering transitioning into or starting a house church.

"This is something we're passionate about and we believe in this model and it'll grow," he said, noting that traditional church attendance is dropping. "God's going to use it."

"It's a powerful movement," he commented. "You can't really put it in a box."

Eastburn was a youth pastor for 13 years and has "done [his] time with the more traditional model" of church, having previously worked at a church plant of Saddleback Community Church – the megachurch of prominent evangelical leader Rick Warren – as well as other churches.

He has nothing against traditional churches or even megachurches and acknowledges that there are many people who could never attend a house church.

But, "if you really get it," he says, "it's hard to go back to anything else."

The Well currently has house churches in Yorba Linda, Brea, Tustin, Huntington Beach and La Mirada.

Since the economic downturn began, six financially stressed churches in various states have sought advice from The Well in California's Orange County. It's a 57-year-old Southern Baptist congregation that quit its $5,000-per-month lease in 2005 and formed what has become a network of five house churches. Sensing a need among financially strapped churches, Pastor Ken

Eastburn in April launched a website – leavethebuildingblog.com – to assure struggling churches there's spiritual life after bricks and mortar.

"We didn't really start out encouraging churches to do this, but people who would hear our story started to contact us over the last year," says Pastor Eastburn, whose church has grown from 50 to 75 members since leaving its rented facility. "If this model is something that works, and if we can help other churches [adopt it], then maybe this is what God has us doing right now."

Churches that are partially or entirely building-free come in a variety of forms:

• One-year-old Origin Community Church meets in a Rocklin, California coffeehouse. Childcare happens in a retrofitted school bus and a motor home parked outside.

• The Outdoor Church, launched last summer in West Virginia's Hampshire County, meets at least once a month on hiking trails, in canoes, or in another adventurous natural setting.

• Cornerstone Community Church in Simi Valley, California is saving millions of dollars by expanding into an outdoor amphitheater rather than a new building

• The Village in Las Vegas, Nevada was warned they were "committing ministry suicide," when they were preparing to leave its 12,000-square-foot rental space in April and worship instead in members' homes.

But Pastor Diamond and The Village, as his nondenominational church is known, have survived. Fifteen homes now hold intimate services twice a month. On other Sundays, they dip into funds previously earmarked for rent and use them for special events and outreach, such as a May block party for local African refugees. Now other church leaders want to know how they might follow suit.

Luke, Chapter 10 gives some very workable principles on church planting that fit in the Philippine culture.

There are three main values I see in each one of us that gives us the potential to saturate our country with God's Word through Simple Church. Let us check them one by one and see how it fits in starting house churches mainly in the community.

If we define house church as an 'extended' family meeting together for mutual edification then our family gatherings fit perfectly. Filipino's uphold family ties to the highest extent, we live close to each other even as individual adults. We love to gather just to have a meal together with the entire clan up to the 4th generation. And what's more surprising is that we do not need to put it in our calendars. It becomes an instinct for us to gather and sit, talk, eat, pray [if you don't mind, or prophesy] and serve. Hmmm...it is S.T.E.P.S. on what to do in a house church meeting. We don't even need to create a program to foster new ideas and stories. We are also good at doing surprises when we meet. We love to talk and...eat. We do not need to create a family, we are family.

We call it 'Bayanihan' in our own dialect. It is a creation of alliances with neighbors and a helping attitude whenever one is in dire need. No one needs to teach us on how to create community, we already have one! Our celebrations such as fiestas, holidays and family reunions speak of how we are created for this idea of simple gatherings. Most Filipino's have traditions, either Holy Friday or All Souls Day. It is a religious event yet most families gather around foods and laughter - it becomes an event that is full of surprises to bond relationships. We're not doing it so much anymore for religious purposes but to have fun. Do you know that we Filipino's are known for the number two happiest people in Asia? And who are number one? Me and my family :-)

We call it "Barkada" or a group of selected friends fits most of what a house church looks like. It is church to the fullest. We normally treat our barkada as our second family next to our own physical one, though sometimes others hope it to be their real family. The value behind this group is simple, "You feel like a family." Added to the word barkada is the word 'pakikisama' which is extending support to our relatives or offering help even to our neighbors who are in need. And "Utang na loob,' meaning a debt of gratitude – or the giving of special favors to the other person regardless of the moral outcome. In simple terms, "we might hate one another yet we still love one another."

Based on this premise, a working house church model for us will look a little different than other house churches in other countries. Even in our country, house churches in different cities and towns with different people and personalities will still look different from one another. Put it this way, I could not do house church with the street people the way I do house church with the professional people. It just doesn't work. I must be resilient and adaptable enough to cater to different people. Like Paul, able to become wherever, whatever and whoever he is with.

Starting a house church movement in a community is only one way of doing it. In this article, several people in my circle of influence have used this approach, and some prove it to be hard [mostly to those who keep asking endless questions about it without doing it], yet to most people it works. The principles and practices behind simple church can only be answered by asking the right questions, "Is it right?" No, "Does it work?" If you believe it is right, then it will work. Not the other way around.

In *Luke 10,* Jesus asked us to be sensitive enough on how to recognize a 'man of peace' in a house. Look for the initial sign: food. "If the man of peace offers you food, eat," He said. Something rings in your head, right? Yes, Filipinos were made for simple church gatherings! We know that wherever we go even just passing by someone who is eating they will gladly invite you to eat with him. We know it's not real hospitality right, but we know also that if the person urges us twice or a third time we better accept his offer for he is serious in his asking.

At times I come to think that Jesus somehow has a Filipino appetite, He came 'eating and drinking.' Most Filipino's love this endless eating. He never came to a house where there is no food. Think about in Matthew's house, they have a party! In Zaccheus' house, still there is party with his 'barkada.' At Simon the Pharisees' house also. Looks like Jesus barkada always has someone celebrating a birthday! And have you recognized that whenever Jesus speaks of God's Word He always likens it to a spiritual food? Huh! Yummy ha. [Matthew 4:4]

Starting several home Bible Studies around the community or village is one of the best ways to start a house church movement in an area. Targeting 3-5 family hosts that are close enough to gather them for the future celebration is an ideal attempt. Leave your 'religious doctrine' behind, but do not forget to bring your 'doctrine of food.'

Honestly, food might be a stumbling block for the family host because they might be out of budget to prepare a meal. But honestly, it is the best way to start a house church. Do some variety next time you come, or ask them not to prepare the next time. Remember, you are going to visit different houses in a day and you don't want to get sick. I tried getting sick because of the different drinks that they offer. I learned my lesson. How To 'Tweak a bit' of your Bible Study method to look like a house church setting: Most of us who are Christians from denominational streams have a way of doing Bible Studies in someone's house. So I included at least five ways you can change your approach.

If possible, the schedule for your Bible Study in these houses can be done only in one day, each can end up for one hour at least to one and a half hour at most including fellowship time.

Take more time asking normal questions such as: "How are you today?" "What have you been doing these days?" and "How's the children?"

Make sure you will not look and sound like a 'heavenly man' especially if you are preparing these families as 'God's own family' on earth as it is in heaven when you finally start a house church. Don't be religious, I mean.

If you can run a 20 - 30 minute 'open Bible discussion' it is great to start with good participation. 'Open Discussion' means that you do not appear to them as one who knows better than anyone else who are present.

Do not talk too much and do not worry if the discussions go off the topic. Be sensitive enough especially if you allow them to ask questions. Remember, most questions the person asks are his own personal struggles inside his heart. Make sure you ask questions that can reveal God's intentions to human illusions.

A couple of 'quick' visits at the family during the week are very helpful to build some rapport. 'Go with flow' might mean sitting with a mother while she's washing clothes or cooking. She might appreciate a helping hand and affirmations from you like one I love: "You look blooming today Nanay, what did Tatay do to you today?" This wife is in the middle of cooking some food for dinner while I gave her a hand helping chops some veggies. The husband sits around watching TV and hears me speak these words and answered teasingly, "Of course, I took good care of my wife." though behind my back they often fight.

As soon as the father affirms my statement I directly admonishes them saying, "That's good because Paul says in the Bible that husbands should love their wives, and wives should submit to their husbands." And both them nod and answered me back, "Really?" And a long discussion ends up having a meal together with them. This does not become a 'quick' visit then but becomes more intimate with the family, which is much better. These kinds of visits are not for 'religious' purposes or to earn their trust for them to go to your church. This is church already, in real life situations.

To reach the unbelievers quick and fast, house churches are the ideal. To encourage believers to attend your house church is the surest way to have a debate, unless he or she is tired enough of doing traditional church. Simple Church then is for non-believing people. You do not need to share to them about a 'holy man dressed in a holy robe, to speak in a holy place for a holy message in a holy day for a holy fee,' as Wolfgang Simson suggests. They know nothing about these matters. In other words, they have no traditional 'garbage' in their mind.

I was once an aggressive house church guy who loved to roam around and whatever Christian person I'm in contact with I would always share enthusiastically about house church and how it is simple enough for anyone to just do it. Honestly, I ended up having big arguments that lasted from 5 in the afternoon to 2 in the morning. I won the argument but lost a friend. Not a good way on 'how to win friends and influence people!'

After that experience, I decided to just be quiet as much as I could but at the same time sensitive enough to listen to their heart's cry. Often they needed a change in the way they do church 'as we know it.' Our level of hunger is not the same as someone else's so we cannot just use the same words that changed us to change other people's hearts.

Christians are saved people already, that's the simple fact. They do not need to be saved again. In the Philippines, there are still 80% of the people who don't really know who Jesus is to them. Let's focus our target to the lost and let Jesus Himself deal with His church about its monthly bills and expensive problems, uh, programs. Let Jesus creates a hunger for reality in His church through its shortcomings.

The job of a church planter is to 'leave' as fast as he can after the house church has been established. Since I started in 2000, only three house churches out of 13 that I established still continue to this day. The problem? I did not prepare others to do what I was doing. A responsible servant of God will not remain in insecurity about the ministry that God has prepared for you, but will give others the permission to do the same. My principle in training is, if I know how to do it, why should I do it? Let him who knows not what to do, do it. For how can he learn if I do it myself? God mostly then will give each of us the work and the work will teach us how to do it.

Jesus sent the disciples 'two by two.' Why? For prayer and encouragement and of course for modeling purposes - learning from each other *[2 Timothy 2:2]*. A good leader leads others only for a while, and the lets the Holy Spirit take charge of his own disciples life and training. The 'natural father,' is trained in real life situations, not as a professional clergyman from the seminary. He first leads his own extended family. Only then can the leader leave and come back once in a while, to see the growing life of the church

A simple success principle: Always bring others with you on the journey.

Church is about relationships, nothing more and nothing less. Loving God, loving your neighbor, and loving your enemy. Stop specializing in some liturgy and special outlines for your Bible Study. But start specializing in building healthy and devoted relationships with each other. You can win a person's heart in a day quicker than a hundred sermons in a year.

In the Philippines, respect and honor can be seen in two ways: When you enter a house 'leave your slippers or shoes' outside and greet. Second, bless the hand of the elderly. Leaving your slippers outside especially if the house is clean can earn you great respect. Though most of the family host doesn't really care, but 'attempting' to do it is a sure way that you are welcomed at their house.

Blessing the hand of the elderly is a Catholic tradition for many years, but not now, at least in the Philippines. Yet it is showing respect to your elders, and parents and Lola's and Lolo's love it. And what in return? The elder's/parents who are in charge pf most of the house will treat you as their son or daughter instantly!

Establishing relationships with the family you're trying to reach out to is vital in the making of a simple church. Why? Church is simply a family. This is the ultimate picture of church in the Bible! God, the Almighty, the God of Abraham, Isaac and Jacob becomes our Father? What a paradigm shift this is. And I became his son? And Jesus became my eldest Son? We are to treat each other as brethren, *I Timothy 6:1-5*. And we are called the 'household of faith?'

Remember, a house church is your extended family. It is a reflection of God's family on earth, as it is in heaven. So learn to be one with them.

How Shall We Then Meet?

When we look closely at the different aspects and effects of certain numbers in group life, the question gets raised as to whether or not these understandings of numerical dynamics can actually help us gather more intentionally.

So rather than being frustrated with different sized groups, when we get to know the dynamics of numbers, it is possible we can really begin meeting more strategically. If permission has been given to do church differently, why would we insist on meeting the same way, with the same format, even the chairs set the same way, in the same room, basically doing the same thing week after week?

Many are feeling significant disinterest with our basic larger weekend gatherings called "church." Some of that sense of disconnect is not at all about the need to gather as the church but the sheer boredom with too many meaningless meetings built around the same old predictable formats of the "song, sit, sermon syndrome," weekend after weekend.

No matter what we do with changing the meeting format, time, place, style, we are still called to get together. The Hebrews 10:25 mandate is interesting in that most translations use the term "assembling ourselves together." For me personally that was always been a put off. The first thing that comes to mind is my old High School assemblies, large meetings where all the students filled the bleachers and the gymnasium floor for some special, usually boring, presentation.

The word is actually best translated "to gather together" (epi-sun-ag-ein). It could mean any number of people, even smaller numbers of people. No set quota of what constitutes a gathering, simply a gathering together.

Jesus uses the same word in talking about eagles (or vultures as some translate) gathering around a body (Luke 17:37), and/or a mother hen gathering her chickens under her wings (Matthew 23:37). It is hard to see large crowds in all of these pictures, with rows of chairs and platforms and programs. It seems more about a gathering around something. Maybe even something more like an intimate circle.

So, yes, we do need to gather or flock together as God's people, and our verse in Hebrews 10 might even point us towards "more often" as we see that Day approaching. We do need to be near each other, in relationship with each other, and in communication with each other in order to do and be the "one another's" so explicitly laid out throughout the New Testament.

Sometimes in our exotic attempts to create new kinds of meetings or new forms or new structures that will bring about that greater new place with each other, we forget some basic principles.

Life in God, in His family, is not about meetings as much as it is about His purposes in a meeting. It is what we are gathered around. It is what He does when we get together, or what He wants to do in the center of each gathering. It is about a connection not just a crowd, it is about affection, about fidelity, a feeling of being gathered around Him as we are gathered with each other.

No new structure will guarantee that, but it is about whatever He has called us to gather around.

Too often doing the same things again and again, giving into the habitual forms of Christian conformity can become a great enemy to true community. If we just go to the same pace and do the same things we assume we will experience community. Not so. It could even be that these kinds of early gatherings at the end of Acts 2 were not even planned meetings but really people caught in the act of being unable to stay away from each other. They just had to keep gathering around their new found life in Christ, and all that that meant.

We know they had a strict cultural Temple model, it shows up in the very next chapter (Chapter 3), as the miracle happens on the way to a certain hour of prayer at the Temple. So I am not so sure that what we see happening in the end of Acts 2 is because of necessarily a newly discovered agenda, a new plan, a new liturgy, a new curriculum, or a new manual, as much as their lives were so radically changed by Jesus, with many unable or unwilling to leave Jerusalem so they simply had to drop in on each other as often as possible to share that wonderful new radical life in God.

They weren't going to house church because of somenewly designed revelation, they weren't going anywhere, they just couldn't stay away from each other's homes, and getting daily involved in each other's lives. Sure, they continued to go to Synagogue or Temple for a while, but Christianity was well on its way to becoming an unstructured lifestyle and growing relationships together rather than some new address to meet at.

We need to pray for one another during these days of transition. Many seem to echo this idea that they feel they are in what might be coming out of a "deconstructionist zone" or even coming through a season of "detox," concerning their prior habits of meeting or gathering with other believers.

In this season the Jeremiah (1:10) wrecking crew is busy "rooting out," "pulling down," "destroying," "throwing down," what seems old, or antiquated, or non effective in the many ways we have gathered and seems to bestirring up a great hunger for the for His Manifest Presence, and a deeper, more authentic community.

I think it feels a whole lot like the first part of the Sunday Night TV Series "Extreme Home Makeover." You know, the part when the existing house or structure gets demolished. The needy family is whisked off to some exotic vacation site as they watch their old house get razed to the ground via computer from a distant site. And then with full speed cooperation, the hyper-construction crews begin the remodel, the rebuild, accomplishing their task in record-breaking time.

Transition seems to always take us to extremes. Either old house or new house, but with so much work in the middle. Kind of like church, either fewer meetings or maybe even too many meetings.

We seem to polarize between extremes of passive isolation, try to survive outside the body in the "just Jesus and me phase," or in the opposite of the frantic addiction to activities as we jet about looking for the next watering hole, the next glory fest, the next angel filled conference, the newest church in town, ad nausea.

We must not become discouraged; this transition of learning to gather differently will take some time. We are carrying a lot of institutional baggage as we have done meetings so many certain ways for so many years. And we don't have to just throw everything out and wing it either. Instead we get to become even more intentional as we hear God's voice together on how we are to now gather.

If we understand that we have the freedom to gather differently in this "permissional time," it means we can experiment with more intentionality and more direction, not less. And that we can actually use what we have learned about different-sized, different-focused gatherings to our advantage as well as God's advancement of His work in us.

We of course could choose by default to let all of our gatherings remain stuck in the "sit, soak and sour," mode of days past, or actually and delightfully and intentionally get God's mind and plan for the different kinds of gatherings He wants to lead us into. He is very willingly to work with us if we will work with Him.

When preparing to gather, go ahead and ask some leading questions. Where are you in your walk with God? Where are you in your relationships with others? So, why are you going to gather with this certain group? Where do you want God to take you, where do you want the night to go? What are you willing to do to get there?

Answers to these kinds of questions may help when you know what it is you are wanting or looking for in a gathering with others.

Try gathering in a smaller group. Maybe even a very small group. Maybe 3 or 4. Gender specific. With the purpose of learning to walk together as deeply committed, trustworthy and authentic covenant friends (Amos 3:3).

Hang out with these friends in such a way that as Neil Cole (Church Multiplication Resources) says in his simple outline, you create a place where sin is confessed in mutual accountability, God's Word is read repetitively in context and community, and souls are prayed for strategically, specifically and continuously.

This kind of intimacy and friendship takes time, and will not be the only meeting you participate in. But it can be a very meaningful part of your growth together with a few others. Start with an hour or each week. over coffee, and watch it grow into spending significant quality time together. In these smaller groups no leader is necessary, no curriculum is necessary, no is workbook necessary and no training is necessary. Just a willingness to grow together and to grow up!

Neil Cole's little pamphlet about these small but powerful Life Transformation Groups on his website at: www.cmaresources.org.

Try simple church with 5 to 15 people gathered around a full meal enjoying the ebbs and flows of life as a family. These cross-generational meals can include everyone, kids and all. We all have to eat; we all enjoy each other's presence. And there during the buzz of the family-like meal we can hear, chat, interrupt, laugh, cry and pray together as an extended family.

When the meeting gets too large and the family-like dynamic changes, make necessary adjustments, and start new groups.

Do projects together, have outings together, go camping and bowling together. Involves the kids in different ways, as you basically enjoy an evening meal together with friends. And all of this can be highly attractive and contagious to your pre-Christian friends and neighbors, so keep some places at the table open for others. You just start by scheduling a meal, inviting others to come, and watch God do the rest.

Find those spiritual warriors in your community who are fighting and winning spiritual battles. The ones who know how to pray, how to see in the Spirit, how to heal the sick and how to operate consistently in the authority of the believer. Basically, if you want to have a prayer gathering, find people who know how to pray.

This army is growing everywhere; start asking where they meet, what they do, and how you can share your specific and strategic needs with them.

These people are involved in intercessory groups; they are technicians with the Healing Rooms. Many are covert, and by no means drawing attention to themselves, and yet their reputations are known by the Spirit.

When you get together with these kinds of strategic people, the strategies will come in the meeting. The prayer direction, the national or international focus points. I heard of one group that watches the news channel and then pauses it when it calls for a strategic kinds of international praying.

Just listen for the sounds; you hear them everywhere these days. From boom boxes to huge sound systems. From iPods to finely-tuned stereos. Sounds of war, sounds of intimacy, sounds of celebration. Thunderous stomps over injustice, sweet, angelic melodious sounds for soaking and contemplation. Wild and crazy sounds that send you leaping and jumping. Romantic, and wooing sounds that have you in tears and silence.

Gather the musicians and singers and dancers around these sounds. Remember when David set aside the 4,000 musicians and the 288 singers to sing before the Lord 24/7. Then take these sounds to the streets, to the city parks, to the apartments courtyards, to the office complexes, to the coffee houses, to the beaches and of course to the cathedrals and chapels. Make room for the spontaneous sounds, not just the pre-learned songs of the day.

Find your own sound that builds with the others. And then give yourself to the full release of your sound, the participation of the instrument that you are. It is more about the sound you carry than your instrumental or musical talent.

What about walking through the Scriptures with some friends, asking freely and openly for insight, revelation and application. Gather a reading group around a certain agreed upon book, or listen to a CD/DVD series and discuss it openly. Even discuss it in public places, like a local coffee shop or a park, or the clubhouse at your apartment complex. Watch the curious interaction with others that God can cause in these open settings.

Gather some of your friends around someone's specific life message. A local teacher or pastor in your community, one of the fathers and mothers in the faith that you all know can be brought into your group for great times of teaching and feedback and interaction.

Have several of these spontaneous gatherings to empower and equip each other. Keep asking God what He wants to say to you, and keep listening, as He will direct you to invite others who carry a certain timely message for your group.

Doing the Kingdom with friends is what Christ modeled for us. Life in God is not meeting-focused, but is relationally lived. The signal most pivotal verse in this season of my life about relationship and connection comes from Mark 3:13,14 as Jesus called the twelve to first be "with" Him, and then second, to "send " them. Whatever you are called to do these days, do it with Jesus and with others.

This is no time to be stingy with creativity; this is no time to be boring or predictable. Do these gatherings with freedom and delight. Do them with new meaning, with bold intention, and radical passion. And don't wait for all of these gatherings to be planned and scheduled by someone else, don't wait for the special announcement to make the Sunday bulletin. Like Nike said, "Just do it."

This is a new day of getting together. It is time to gather and pursue deep authentic faith communities all over our region as we celebrate our Creative Creator.

Is It House Church Yet?

One might surmise by the sheer numbers that we have an international House Church movement on our hands, right? Isn't this what we have been waiting for? Or are statistical numbers deceiving? Even within Third Day Churches we are indirectly related now to hundreds of House Churches in thirteen nations. But is this the House Church movement we have been waiting for?

In some of these countries it just might be. Maybe countries like China and India, but you still wonder whether we are speaking the same language when we say House Churches in North America.

With so few patterns mandated to in Scripture concerning what the "church" is supposed to do, or what it is supposed to look like when it gathers, *(Acts 2; I Corinthians 14; Hebrews 10)* no wonder we are still fussing and feuding over the practices, the central concepts, and constantly questioning if we have actually hit pay dirt.

Even if we believe in the simplest sequences of the First Century Acts Church *(Acts 2:42 - 47)*, the (1) Staying in the Apostle's Teaching, the (2) Fellowship, the (3) Breaking Bread, and the (4) Prayers, there are still many loose ends to be so definitive as to say, "Now that is what Church is supposed to be like."

For example, with no Bibles, how did they exactly stay in the Apostle's Doctrine? How many Apostles were needed to get around to the gatherings that were happening daily from house to house? What exactly was the Apostle's Doctrine or Teaching at such a young stage of development in the early church? Was there a script; a systematic outline? Were there agreed upon guidelines? Or was it a story, His story? And who exactly was allowed to pass along the Apostle's teachings or stories?

There had not been an adequate amount of time to formally call for church hierarchy or protocol, so were the simple saints freed to pass along the stories about Jesus? Things at this early point were not clear. Everything seems pretty fluid, at least until around 180 A.D. when some major institutionalism began to set in.

And where or when did they do these things that the they are caught doing in Acts 2? It says that most of these daily events happened in their homes? How long did this practice go on? How long did these meetings continue with such openness and primitive obedience? Or when did they get more refined or more defined? And what did that look like? And what should it look like today?

Up to a point, as Jon Zens points out, the early church was marked by the manifestation of a polyform ministry with mutual edification and the meeting of needs being accomplished through the gifts of all the brethren, all the saints, all the time.

The post-apostolic church would eventually move more and more towards a separate ministry for certain gifts, eventually even a limited clergy, but not in the beginning. This baby church was pretty much a lively, large family of faith, where every meeting was full of serendipitous moments of freedom and expression with all the priesthood of believers participating.

This early expression, was an exploding, full-blown, one-another operation in the homes of all of the believers. It functioned everyday, all the time, with miracles and meals flowing, and with so many people getting saved only God could count them (Acts 2:47).

Robert Lund notes, "*This was the perfect plan to accomplish the explosive growth that came from the good news being spread throughout the land. With the priesthood of all believers, explosive Holy Spirit growth, God dwelling in each person, an obvious and constant shifting from stable to dynamic growth, and a persistent emphasis on interpersonal relationships, no wonder the early Christians chose homes to be the focal point of all of their gatherings.*"

Can you even imagine the buzz in the city? 3,000 newly baptized believers *(Acts 2:41)*, and then soon another batch of 5,000 *(Acts 4:4)?* What was going on in the atmosphere around Jerusalem with thousands of brand new believers in Yeshua literally everywhere you looked?

Meeting, laughing, talking, healing, eating, fellowshiping, worshiping. Can we even begin to think of this growth in our classic discipleship paradigms? I can imagine the questions going on inside you head right now. Who was cleaning the fish? Who was teaching the basics? Come to think of it what are the basics? Who leads what? What was the most important thing they did when they met?

A New Kind Of House Church Movement

I realize that when I think of the term "house church," especially in consideration of these first few chapters in Acts, that I am referring to something far different than our current preoccupation. It seems like our main goal is to get today's weekend crowds out of our bigger buildings where they are being warehoused each weekend into our smaller, homier ones. But a whole lot more than that was going on in these early chapters of the Bible.

We have to start thinking back, before we can ever thinks forward. We have to think more of the church of God, or the people of God as being freshly lit by the fire of the Holy Spirit, incredibly empowered and released into their neighborhoods, people groups and cities, like a wildfire, taking God's life, God's power, and His living transforming Spirit from one person to the next until the whole community literally explodes.

What seems to reappear, again and again, is that every time we read these early expressions of Christianity we see its rawness. So raw, that this living church, this body of believers, simply cannot be contained.

It cannot be boxed into a house or a sanctuary. It is so alive, as to be out of control, at least man's control. To review the effect of these fire-filled people on their early culture, is to recognize that God never intended us to build fireplaces, (places to house the fire) whether they are large ones or small ones, but to release this firestorm called His church to blaze throughout the land.

If we are not careful in our so-called house church movements, we might just be doing greater damage than the legacy church movement. By simply trying to box these fires into even smaller fireplaces in our folksy little homes and apartments, are we snuffing out the blaze?

Whether gathered or scattered, it appears sure that these primitive groups were both very simple and very alive. Being cautious that any formatting of our meetings doesn't end up putting out the fire and quenching the power-filled priesthood of the saints, how do we "keep the home fires burning?"

When I ask leaders these days about whether they are actually doing "house churches," I usually know the answer I am going to get.

"Oh yes, they say, we have a bunch of Bible Studies." Which really means that everything they are doing still comes from the select, elite clergy. They have just as many Bible Studies as they have full-time, professionally trained staff, because those individuals are the only ones allowed to lead the Bible Studies. So each staff pastor, if he wants to kill himself, can probably lead four or five per week.

But that is not what I am talking about when I speak of a House Church or a House Church movement. I am talking first of all about a generation of self-feeders, with all the believers growing in Christ, rather than everyone living dependently on a few others to bring them the baby food and the milk bottles of the Word each week.

Believers, both young and old, so on fire and so empowered by a living relationship with the God of the Word that every time they gather the Word pops out, it becomes flesh, and gets worked out as all the believers operate in the "doing " of the Word, rather than just sitting passively, waiting for another "hearing" from some well-intended specialist.*

*(**A Format Reminder:** *With the different kinds of groups God puts us in these days, make sure that the goal is to provide a safe place for people to talk. Whether we are reading the Scriptures, reading a book, finding a topic to spring from, or doing some worship with on our iPods, the goal is the same. The goal of "doing church, differently," is to pursue the freedom and participation of the priesthood of believers, with everyone bringing what they have to the group to toss it into the mix. We ask questions that help lead people to discussion. We lead by listening, not lecturing).*

We all know the church is not a building. We all know that church is not an event that takes place on Sundays. We all know that when the Scripture speaks of "church," it means a living community. Or as John Eldredge shares (Waking The Dead), "the little fellowships of the heart." These anointed outposts and functioning platoons of the Kingdom.

We all know that the church is about people. People whose lives have been so radically changed by an encounter with the Living God, that they have to get together, they have to worship, they have to pray for one another, they have to hang out together, they have to be involved in each others lives. And when they gather they experience the full impact of the Kingdom of God in every gathering as constantly witness signs, wonders and transformed lives.

They live within a missional-adventure-partnership-with-God-and-each-other. They live this way because they are so on fire. Yes, we each have our own journey, but we also have our shared adventure, and are called to experience a collective journey as the larger fire rages out of control.

We cannot try to shape it, to form it, to name it, or even label it. It is too hot! Every time we get together the fires burns differently, unplanned, unscripted, unhinged, and unpredictable. And every time we scatter, the new quest is freshly empowered, re-ignited, re-charged, because we have been with each other.

I wonder sometimes if we have ever been a part of a true House Church, at least for a very long period of time. I do think I have received glimpses of the real deal. I do think I have had moments in gathering with other believers, in loving them, and in supporting them, and them loving and supporting me that it felt very much like true community, like a real family, like real, authentic church.

But too often I think that when trained gatherers, or people who have been churched too long get into a House Church, with all our baggage, with all our history, with all our stuff, with all our habits, we seem to mess things up by our old habits.

Do we think that a true House Church is what we Christians normally do when we get together in a home once a week? Where we gather to share a meal, to sing some songs, to pray a little, or have a Bible Study? We have all been to a lot of those. But is that House Church? Or is that still just a little Church in a House?

What if "House Church," as Frank Viola indicates (Reimagining Church), is different than that. What if "church," period, is simply a group of Christians living in radical, shared community under the Headship of Christ? What if "church" is actually the mystery of Christ as it is revealed through how a group of people live out their lives together.

And not just in a weekly meeting, but all of the time, and not just with a few finely trained House Church leaders, but with no set pastors, or ministers, titled or untitled. Instead, what if all the members of the gathering gather under Christ's Headship alone? And what if a good test that you are in a true "house church," might be whether or not you can easily pick out the leader?

What if "church" is people learning to live by the Divine Life that is in Christ alone, finding through the discovery of the Spirit each time they gather the most creative way to express that life with each other, day after day, week after week, living out their grand mission, to incarnate Christ's person and purpose to their world?

What if all the members are learning to see and treat each other like a full family, with fathers and mothers and brothers and sisters, who are pursuing the highest good for each other, and taking genuine care of one another? What if handling challenges and difficulties like strong families is what we are called to do?

And what if each smaller group is being called to be a part of something bigger than the group itself by connecting with itinerant apostolic workers within a New Testament pattern or network and support? And what if each group is leaning to live in autonomy while learning to fully identify with the church in the region, as well as the church in the house?

Pitfalls of the House Church Movement

Give me a mop . . .someone's about to spill some wine. Not intentionally, mind you. His church is "transitioning" again. This time into a network of house churches. It's the next thing. The new model. Latest trend. He says. And some people are going to leave and not come back. Consider it collateral damage. A sacrifice. The price you pay for the change. For the next step.

A decision towards progress that is too much, too soon, too hard, too costly. The straw that breaks the camel's back. The choice that pleases some and sends others away. People leave the church as turtles or skunks. This is what Brother Thomas Wolf told me. Turtles crawl quietly out the back door, without bringing attention to the protest of their silent withdrawal. Skunks leave at the front, where everyone can see them, where they can let everyone know how badly they will be missed, how they should have been listened to. They leave a smell behind that lasts a lifetime. A stinky reminder of the decision that divided.

And the Sanctuary of the Wineskin sees the light of day. Opens to the elements. Wine spills. Through the cracks. Runs in the streets like blood, searching for a new home. Is God happy?

Despite the vocal crowd who worship at the Cult of the New, Jesus is not infatuated with new wineskins. He likes both. But He is a connoisseur of vintage wine. Mature wine. Wine that has sat under time, ripened, grown, perfected under the conditions. Wine like this is achieved only by permitting the new containers and preserving the old ones. Let the old wineskins be preserved. If you squirt fresh wine into them, they will burst. Spill. Jesus doesn't like spillage. Jesus likes mature wine. So we need wineskins also. Old wine in the old wineskins. New wine in the new wineskins. Whatever. Whatever keeps it. Contains it. Preserves it. Gives it room to move and expand. Grow into what it is destined to be and securing it from disease. Both. Freedom and safety. Creativity and security. Bubbly and still. The heights of exploding taste and the depths of softened character. Flavor and body. Cherries and oak. Cheekiness and gracefulness. The wabi and the sabi. The vigor of youth and the wisdom of age. Both, says Jesus. Both. Both will be preserved.

But here is the challenge: To allow the new without threatening the old. To preserve the old without hindering the new. Those without wisdom choose one but not both. And the result is skunks and turtles.

I visited a House Church in the early 90's. It was run by skunks. A group of disgruntles whose happiness came from the fact they met on Thursday and not Sunday. In a living room and not a sanctuary. On a sofa and not a pew. They were like kids staying away from school, hiding out, proud of their boldness to leave. And yet in all their freedom they managed only to move the church service from a building to a house. Not much else had changed. Only the location. They had the smirks of naughty boys on their faces. They were a church service on the run. An escaped meeting captured by a living room. One that built its identity from rebellion, defined themselves by what they were not. This was the Revenge of the Skunks. I didn't go back to that church. But I have been hanging out with turtles.

"They're not organized" insists the Owner in the movie "Chicken Run". But she is wrong. The chickens have been cooped up long enough. They build a plane and fly over the fence. To a new world. An island. To set up a new existence away from tyranny. To become Free Range Chickens. Free Range Turtles, on the other hand, left quietly and by themselves. No machinery. No noises. Just a quiet withdrawal. A velvet revolution. Pilgrimage. A solitary exodus. Their tithes first and then their attendance.

Their protest was in their feet. They choose not to come back but still kept up relationships with those who stayed. Lest they be like the skunks.

But on their journey outside the institution, some of them discovered each other. Ate meals with each other. Prayed with each other. More often. More regular. Sometimes weekly. Those with gifts gave them. Those with abilities used them. Those with leadership led. Those with wisdom taught. Those who liked the way things were going told others. New churches emerged in places where Turtles lived. This was now the Time of The Turtles. Neighbors and friends got caught up. Church people thought it peculiar. New believers thought it quite normal. The kind of thing they would do if they had to make a church. Why not in a home? A coffee shop? Wherever people live? Isn't that how the first church did it in the Bible?

These were another group. Not skunks or turtles. Another. Butterflies, perhaps. No rebellion. No scars. No issues with ecclesiastical entities. Just people who liked to live with each other in each others context. Environments with wallpaper and photos and TV magazines. Lives located somewhere. Homes where people live and children pick their noses and dogs annoy. Real people who want to see deeply into each other's lives. To delight in the beauty. To heal what is broken. To be healed. Touched. Appreciated but not used. Perhaps these people are the third wave. People who church together without contrasting. Part of a church without an address. A movement without a label . For they do not always call what they do "house church". Sometimes there is no house. Even "home church" does not contain their experience of God and each other in this covenanted journey.

But back to the Pastor-man who is about to rupture his church. He has probably heard the current criticisms about the house church movement. "No leadership," they say. "Prone to heresy," they say. "An incubator for cults. They don't last. No leadership." They say.

They say wrong! Tyranny thrives in a vacuum of passivity. Finds its voice inside an intimidated silence. It cannot live under the lively chatter of dinner-table conversation. Dictators cannot bully themselves to the front when leadership is valued by character instead of rank, and is distributed out to the right people for the right moment. Like ducks flying in formation, until the change, when another duck takes the lead for the present direction. Ducks have leadership. Just not the One Leader who leads all the time. And for every thing. And every direction. My pastor friend has the answers for the wrong complaints. He should listen to what is really wrong with the House Church movement. From people within it. From those road-testing the new models. Kicking the tires. He should listen to me. Because I have some gripes about the House church movement. I need to vent them. And he needs to hear them. Here they are:

First and foremost, house churches have no sex appeal. There is nothing to look at. No big event. No climactic happening that makes people snap pictures. Except people crying on each other. Hugging on each other. Although some people would say that those personal victories ARE the story. Wolfgang Simson said that to me last month. I remember the good old days of church planting the old fashioned way. The glory days of toys and more toys. Picking out mega-wattage sound systems. Shopping for electronics. Designing kick-butt graphics for the invitation. Discovering the building. Raising the money. The gut-twisting suspense of Opening Service. The relief of the big crowd that came. Those lovely, dear people that came. God bless 'em, everyone! And then the disappointment of the smaller crowd the following week. And the week after. And the week after that. The grief of losing steam. The guilt of swiping people from other churches to replace those horrible, spiteful deserters who came the first week to see the big fuss and then left forever. Stood us up. Not caring for our feelings. Or our budget. And after all we did for them . . . OK. Maybe the memories are not all fond. But I do miss the hormone-triggering excitement of pulling off a big service. And then on the other hand, if I am really honest with myself, some house church people are beginning to host large city-wide celebrations and be more involved in the week long festivals. In fact I have been to some really good ones.

All right. My first gripe is not going the way I wanted it to. But the following gripes are actual real-life insufficiencies that need to be addressed if house church spokespeople are to offer a viable alternative to pastors leaving the Pyramids Of Egypt for The Good Land Flowing With Milk And Coffee.

The focus needs to change from "Our House" to "Their House" Much of the present house church movement is still an attempt to contain and control the meetings in their own camp, in this case OUR HOUSE. The full gains that are available will not be realized until we can begin to let the movement flow into THEIR HOUSES. The church in Lydia's house was just that - in Lydia's house. Matthew's party was in Matthew's house. Not the more convenient house of Simon

Peter's mother-in-law. And don't tell me it was her stomach complaints that kept them away. It was strategy, not dysentery, that led them to Matthew's house. Jesus told his missionaries to put peace on THEIR (those other people, the ones they were sent to) HOUSE, enter their house, live in their house, eat in their house, heal someone or something in their house. Right there is the base of a new church and it is in THEIR house. Think of the benefits.

Financial, because if the party is in their house then they pay for it. Security, because if the party is in their house then they will guarantee everyone is safe. Culture, because the friends of the host already appreciate the culture of their style of music and culture so there is no culture barrier Convenience, because they already have that house. Etc. I could go on. I could also say that this principle needs to be applied on the civic level as well as the domestic level. That the city offers a gift to those who receive it.

The label needs to change from house church to something that better describes it. The house church network in Prague started 6 months ago. People meet in many different venues but none meet in a house. People there cannot afford a house. "Home church" is better but they don't always meet in homes. Clubs? Yes. Dunkin' Donuts? Yes. Apartments? Sometimes. Neil Cole called them Simple Churches. I like that. Organic Church. Micro church. . . More work needs to be done here.

And what about the rapid movement of monastic structures in the evangelical church in UK and USA? These intentional residential communities are more house-based than the house churches and yet we don't call them house churches. Do we include them under the umbrella term or allow them to define themselves under a whole new ecclesiastic framework?

Another spanner in the works. I visited a "traditional" church in Minneapolis called Solomon's Porch. 200 people meet in a large loungy space with couches, carpets, and sprawling kids. Their service is more housechurch-like than some house churches. What is wrong with this picture? Probably the words being used to describe it.

Hey, look at me, I'm griping.

House churches are not recognized by the mainstream. "They are not real churches", a well-known American pastor told me. He was basing his judgment on the old way of valuation, the "Cold War" mindset Thomas Friedman called it, where people value weight, size and longevity. In the information age, people value things by "Speed". Bill Gates said it was "Velocity". If this is correct, then house churches make a lot of sense. And if 9-11 has moved us out of the Information Age and into the Security Age, then house churches make even more sense. Time for a little Rodney Dangerfield Respect to flow towards house church.

In the meantime, don't expect authentication from the mainstream. The house church movement is basically overlooked and downgraded. Denominational executives are threatened by the idea of housewives starting churches in their own homes rather than their trained professionals in the buildings that were designed for this purpose.

Yes, there are exceptions. The Baptist General Convention of Texas, for example, when they discovered that a house church network in their own backyard had grown into 250 churches within 6 years, decided to take what they had learned and release it all over Latin America. Fantastic. But the mainstream American church is either not ready or not that interested at the moment. "Call back later when you start some real churches." Yeah. I'm really griping now. Stand back. I have some more.

House churches are the cookie dough of the new ecclesiology. They are tasty and soft and very tempting. But they have not yet hardened into something permanent. We might be 5 years away from seeing a complete ecosystem of organic ministries that work together to enable a healthy, reproducing, movement of house churches. The movement in USA and Europe is not ready for franchising or exporting, It is not looking for entrepreneurs to multiply it but rather for pioneers to beta test it. For engineers who can tinker with it while it is moving. To make it workable and efficient. To get the bugs out of the system. To see what missing elements need to be included.

Perhaps God is not allowing recognition from the mainstream so that there can be a window of time to create the prototypes away from the spotlight. If this is correct, someone needs to get busy working on a decent support system. There is not a whole lot of support for the movement right now. Not enough, perhaps, for most pastors to seriously consider a leap of faith into a new and way-more-organic paradigm. A few good books have appeared. Some helpful conferences started up in 2001. The launch of House 2 House magazine is a good start. But the house church movement in Western countries is still a few tuna casseroles short of the potluck.

The five-fold ministry teams are not yet in place. City-wide gatherings are still in the idea phase. The apostles and prophets are still learning how to put up with each other, let alone minister together. Traveling teams are more novelty than staple. The heroes of house church planting are somewhere in Asia.

What about resources from the mainstream church? Sorry. Wrong number. Their conference speakers have not written any books on how to ignite house church movements of the Spirit. Seminaries are not training students to plant house churches. Churches train their youth to "find" a church when they leave for college rather than "start" a church, since the existing structure is too complex for students to replicate. There is also a tragic separation between traditional church and house church. Which leads to my last gripe.

House Church Utopia is still painted as being pure and contaminent-free. As if you leave one model of church and adopt another with no reference to what you came out of. The truth is that there is compromise. There are house church people that miss the worship service so much that they create one.

There are people that go back monthly to visit friends. There are house churches that are more structured than some "traditional" churches. There are large churches that have house churches and large worship services inside their structure and they are very happy with it. This is not a case of Mac OS versus Windows. It is not always either/or. It is more of a progressive evolution. And fish with legs are a reality of this new movement.

Backwash happens. And its OK. If we don't allow more fluidity into what we promote as house church, then a whooooole lot of wine is gonna get spilled as pastors move their churches towards Housopia and discover along the way that 100% Organic certification is just not attainable.

Somebody, somewhere, needs to give people a little slack. Some space to be pluralistic. Someone needs to integrate the new history and the new structure with the previous generation of churches. To stand on their shoulders rather than slap their cheeks. The Holy Spirit utilized the old-school Festival of Pentecost to kick off something new. The disciples launched out from the Temple. Paul started in synagogues. Why can't the house church leaders be players in the wider picture of what God is doing among the old AND new wineskins?

OK. Thanks for letting me vent. Final thoughts? Lets all just get along. Lets be honest about where we are in this transition. Lets not spill any wine. Lets not spoil the fun of pastors surfing the previous wave. Lets preserve the old wineskins and birth the new ones. Lets watch the return of the Turtles. Lets work towards House Church 1.2. Or 2.0. Or 3.5 And then I can stop griping.

Seating – comfortable Bathroom Proximity - always close Music - if its a multi-room party No sermon - teaching is interactive DIY Potential - anyone can do it Size - small is intimate Cuisine - bring on the love feast Freedom of Movement - room-floating encouraged Security - less likely a bomb target Speed - it could happen tonight

Seating - no back pew to hide on Bathroom Proximity - everyone notices Music - if its an attempt at cum-by-ya No sermon - if you're are a preacher DIY Potential - if you want to be a paid professional Size - small is bad for babe-scouting Cuisine - No more potlucks in the church hall Freedom of Movement - expect to be interrupted by the dog Security - who took my CD's? Speed - it could happen tonight in your house

Mission House Churches

"The harvest truly is plentiful, but the laborers are few." (Matthew 9:37)

A standing concern over the recent emphasis on housechurching, especially with its strong emphasis on the need for deeper fellowship and more authentic community, is that we might be once again concentrating too much on those already saved, fixated on catering to their emotional, social and edification needs, getting too ingrown, becoming less missional, and ignoring the enormity of the Great Commission and today's harvest.

Some might even warn us, that the Scripture says to, *"Pray to the Lord of the Harvest,"* (Matthew 9:38) not, *"Pray to the Lord of the Fellowship."* So, is there a sense of caution here about too much fellowship, too much navel gazing, too much community?

I don't think that the emphasis on housechurching is a Great Commission problem if we constantly rethink the goal of fellowship, the goal of community. When we remind ourselves that purpose of gathering as believers is mutual edification *(Hebrews 10:24, 25)*, and the exposure to the multi-faceted giftings of a local body then the exposure to true and authentic community actually can help produce happier and healthier saints. Who in turn are naturally more effective as living witnesses to their world.

I have wondered for a long time whether our classic emphasis on *Matthew 28; Mark 16, Luke 24; John 20; Acts 1* and the *Great Commission* has been all that effective in motivating people to evangelize effectively. I do believe in a Great Commission, in The Great Commission, and I desire deeply an empowered, living community of faith that embodies and incarnates that message of Jesus to the world.

I just wonder how much of the power of that message comes through the latest evangelism trend, over-zealous evangelists or by being rightly related to our Heavenly Father and to His people; the body of Christ?

For years as a city pastor I attempted to do everything in my power to help create the kind of unity that would emulate *Psalm 133* and fulfill Christ's High-priestly prayer in *John 17*. Wondering all along if we would actually have a greater impact on our culture if we got caught truly in love with God and with each other?

A reread of Jesus' prayer might reveal a different focal point, "*that they all may be one, as You Father are in me,*" *(John 17:21)*. Is it possibly putting a greater emphasis on the relationship of intimacy and oneness between Jesus and His Father first, rather than the exclusive inference to the horizontal one of fellowship unity between you and I. First of all, with worldwide Christianity now boasting 37,000 denominations, what a daunting task this horizontal unity presents. I am simply thinking out loud as to whether we may have overstated the horizontal part of this unity and may have missed the greater vertical intimacy that will be followed by the fruit of the horizontal oneness. I do know this, that when the vertical relationship between my Father and I is intact, that automatically sheds light and dynamic on my horizontal relationship with others.

I also know that when my relationship of intimacy is broken with the Father it creates a very difficult environment for any true or meaningful fellowship with one another. I have come to call this the "sucking sound of fellowship."

Get some Christians together who do not have a working personal history with God, and their need for community is out of proportion, out of balance, and it screams "community" when the actual need is for intimacy with their personal God to be restored. The migration Christians from fellowship to fellowship is more likely a pilgrimage or search for Him rather than for each other. As we pursue Him, our love, our patience, and our way of being with each other radically changes.

I guess what I am saying goes back to my past reference on the classic sequence of Jesus in His own personal ministry in *Luke 6:12 - 19*. It seems there was a very distinct purpose to the sequential priorities in the life of Christ. **(1)** He spent the night in solitude *(intimacy)* with the Father, **(2)** the morning in fellowship *(community)* with His friends, and then **(3)** the afternoon in healing and deliverance *(evangelism)* with the harvest.

I have experienced much inward turmoil over these priorities in my life. So much of my ministry life in the early days was spent in neglect of that Secret Place/Sacred Space with Poppa. Even my fellowship with others that was spotty at best. Much of that seasons was consumed with serving God by serving others, all under the guise of serving the needs of the institutional church.

In the end, I outwardly may have achieved the success of numerical growth, but inwardly I lacked a deep fellowship with God, and a deep friendship with others. I always seemed to muster adequate vision beyond me, giving myself to missions, and to outreach in it many forms, only finding the emptiness in doing without knowing the Father or being really known by my brothers and sisters.

Back to the sequence of *Luke 6*, or what I call the Cadence of Christ. When these priorities are in order, things seem to be different. So let me go even further than the just the concern for too much fellowship. I think the priorities are even different than that. First, we spend time, much time with the Father, then time, deep time, with our friends, not just doing church business, but living in healthy community. And the results of this living in God and with each other will make a far more effective influence on the Harvest field around us.

I do want to work harder at being more intentional in my inclusion of the lost in my daily life, but when the mission overrides my relationships with God and my brothers and sisters, I am destined for burnout or bitterness.

I am more and more convinced that the best outreach comes through a life that is fulfilled up in **upreach** *(To God)* satisfied in **inreach** *(To the saints)* and then released in **outreach** *(To the lost).*

Given that scenario, I want to jump into this new year, and this new season committed to pursuing a new generation of healthy sons and daughters and healthy brothers and sisters who can better reach a lost and drifting society.

Our need is not slicker, more media-savvy approaches to evangelism. The message of Jesus' redemption is clear; the gospel is and always will be the Good News. The message will not change but it can be seen clearer and better and more distinct when we live it out with God and each other.

We are still "in this world," we are still exhibit A, to make the message more believable by how we live.

Or as Daniel Oudshoorn writes,

"Therefore, if the western Church hopes to be missional, it must learn to speak Christianly in the midst of Babel. Instead of changing the gospel message the Church must proclaim the gospel in its original form and allow the way it lives to interpret that message. The Christian message cannot simply

be employed to provide Christian living with cultural approval. Instead Christian living, coupled with faith in the Holy Spirit, ought to provide the content and meaning of the Christian message. When Christianity is proclaimed in this way then the Church will be equipped to reveal a radical new way of being human in the midst of a western culture.

It is the indwelling and embodiment of the Christian story that makes it comprehensible (and perhaps even appealing) to society. It is the actions of the Christian community that exegete the Christian message."

I have always wanted to be more prophetic than I am, often desiring those laser-beam, precision, end-times words that everyone seems to be seeking. Especially today with the whole world in turmoil. So I am sorry, this is such a simple word.

Our finest hour is in front of us, and we will be up for it as we learn to take "baby steps," in living out our faith. A simple return to the main and the plain of loving God and serving one another by meeting the most of basic of needs in front of us, will return us to the potency and power of our message.

Begin by returning to the Father, carving out huge chunks of time, just learning to sit and rest in His presence. Secondly, keep living a life that moves towards authentic community, spending good amounts of time in deeper fellowship with one another, enjoying life as family, as we learn to gather, to eat, to share, to laugh, to pray together, and to genuinely care for each other.

Guaranteed, when we do this, our souls will be filled, our lives will be enriched, and the message of Jesus Christ will gain a great credibility in the eyes and ears of our skeptical culture.

As we shared in February's newsletter, a standing concern of us over the recent years of emphasis on housechurching and community, is that if we are not discerning and careful, we can get so ingrown, so addicted to loving our intimate fellowship, that we might forget to be missional, to go beyond us, and possibly even deftly ignore the enormity and the timeliness of the God's Great Commission and today's ripe harvest.

But, I also have the greatest of hope, that in moving towards the more authentic living of our faith in our homes, in our neighborhoods, and in our daily lives, we might be able to steer more effectively towards the lost and steer away from some of the great mistakes that have been made by believers in the past in trying to reach those who do not yet believe.

When my family and I arrived in the Bay Area of Northern California over thirty years ago, we came into the city God had called us to at a time when the entire nation was in the throws of one of the most extensive campaigns it had seen to date. "Here's Life America," was a multi-million dollar evangelistic effort sponsored by Campus Crusade for Christ, originally founded by Bill Bright.

It was localized in 253 major metropolitan regions of the United Sates, involving no less than 14,500 local congregations across the country.

It was claimed that during that crusade three-fourths of all Americans were exposed to the campaign's catchy slogan, "I Found It." You could see it on bumper stickers, billboards, and massive television commercials everywhere.

Without question, North American churches had joined together into what was perceived as a quantum leap forward in the attempted evangelism of this nation.

At the end of the day though, when it was over, all indications were, that whereas "Here's Life America," was a streaming media success, it had proved to be a drastic evangelistic failure. As the facts of all the empirical studies came in, it saw merely a trickle of new members actually added to the body of Christ, with some experts concluding that this massive effort had virtually no measurable impact on church membership in the United States.

Somehow, something deep, something core, something essential had been forgotten. It was the simplest reality that when a person comes to faith, or commits his or her life to Christ, ultimately they do so for reasons that are important to that individual person.

The reasons may not seem vital to that one's family, to that one's friends, even to that loving friend who is endeavoring to lead that person to faith. But the final reasons are deeply essential and critical to that individual who decides to commit their life to becoming a follower of Jesus.

Experts call the reasons people do things, "motives." And because it is generally premature to ask someone to do something unless you first understand how he or she feels and thinks, it seems clear that we may have to be willing to put aside our reasons why our friend should become a Christian and try to see into their world, and try to understand their needs, before we offer the greatest of solutions to all of life's problems.

One of the saddest parts of today's church is that for the most part it has become hidden from life, locked weekly into the four walls of our "stained-glass" wombs, and not available to be seen, witnessed and experienced in the everyday, and interacted with in the normal context of a person's life.

Like some kind of weird "witness protection" system, we have hidden the most powerful witness of the Good News of Jesus Christ, the very people that Christ has changed, filled and empowered to live His life in the world.

People simply do not hear our answers to questions that they have not yet asked for themselves. Any canned presentation, even by the most well meaning Christian towards some hypothetical, average person is like trying to selling tickets on the Ark to someone who has been praying for rain for two years.

The church is to be the visible expression of Christ in this world. It is to be in view of the others. So that by watching or viewing the church, people absorbed as a body of believers, other people can sense, can feel, and can even ask questions. The world must experience the living fullness of Christ.

That is why living church 24/7 in a real world, out in front, for all to examine and to see is so critical. The church is an eternal presence in a fallen, temporal world, but we must have influence. And if all we do is go to meetings, whether in a building or a home, and never interact in the context of others, we have very little influence.

As Dena Brehm once stated, "Just by way of observation preaching was done to those who didn't yet believe, dialogue was done with those who did already believe." When we preach down to others, rather than live in front of them, we keep them at the distance of their unbelief. When we eat with them, laugh with them, cry with them, and most of all listen to them, we become a bridge into their world rather than a disjointed, disconnected religious wedge of condemnation.

When we listen to others we find out what is really going on in that person's life. Then, and only then, we might be able to offer some help to where they are. Even better, we might even be specifically asked to help, at which point the Gospel the Good news of Jesus alive in me has become attractive.

Evangelism is not a course, not a subject, and not a goal. Loving people is. Loving people until they ask "why." Our primary relationship to those outside the faith is not to try to get them to come to a meeting, endure a lengthy sermon and walk the aisle to an altar call. It is to do good works, helping them with any needs that they may have. Whether that be babysitting for them, helping them find a job, or simply having them over for coffee and listening as a friend.

So, how can we do that when we are constantly running off to meetings, even meetings to better learn how to share our faith? How can we do that as we continue to hide behind the excess of our religious activities? As it has been well said, "Preach the good news to everyone, everywhere you go, and when necessary, use words."

"We have too many high sounding words, and too few actions that correspond to them." - Abigail Adams (1744 - 1818)

That is why I so love doing church in a natural way, in a natural setting like a home, an apartment, a yard, a park, an office, in the marketplace of life. And with real people in real-life situations. By observation our neighbors see what goes on, even hear what is going on, long before we try to pounce on them with the "sinner's prayer." The fact that we have time to spend with them, the fact they are not made to feel like the objects of our evangelistic zeal, but rather friends, friends we like being with, and friends we actually care about goes much further than our quick wit with the Four Spiritual Laws or the Roman Road.

What is missing for many people, who might normally be curious about the Christian life, is they don't get to see the Christian "life." They only get to see us going off to another Christian "meeting." They need to be exposed to how we live, how we struggle, and how God continues to transform in the midst of the same difficult circumstances that the whole world lives in.

When we live out this 24/7/365 Christian life, and live it next door, and even invite those neighbors in to participate, we have created a context that makes what we have to offer real. At the end of the day, we only have one thing. We don't need to compete with the world's intellect, music, style, wealth or lack thereof.

We have a unique commodity. The living, breathing example of changed, transformed lives. And seeing them, live, care, cry, struggle, share, hurt, heal, all is part of the picture.

So, lets get about the business of "being the good news," before we attempt to present or proclaim "the good news." Evangelism is a conversation, not a sermon. It is a proactive interaction not a pedantic put-down. It is a series of inclusive acts, not a pattern of rejection or manipulation to adhere to a list of rules.

Jesus was a "friend of sinners." Now does that describe today's kind of Christianity that is only known for its objections and political judgment?

Let's keep the conversation going, keep the neighbors coming, and let's include them now, even before they "pray the prayer," so that we understand they will very likely "belong before they believe."

Finally, let's be reminded that part of God's corporate mission for us is that we would live in transforming communities. Communities that not only feel like family, but act like family when the going gets tough, especially when it is time to confront a brother or sister, and walk them through the "hard times."

Andy Christopher on community recently wrote, "Though community is to be sought after, it should not take the place of a real reverence for the Lord and a respect for His prerogative to reach down and blow up whatever plans we cook up together outside of His specific command."

Changed lives, intertwined with other changed lives, living for the world to see. What a concept of a missional community!

The Attraction of Church

It was a regular Monday morning for me. At least it started out that way. I was sitting in the patio area of a local restaurant in San Diego enjoying my breakfast and reading through the paper. Actually I have made a habit for years of praying through the USA/Today Newspaper in the mornings. What I mean is that I pray the paper by simply reading it and allowing the Holy Spirit to stir anything I read and let it move my heart and spirit towards intercession.

I have always chosen the USA/Today as it gives me the National/International stuff to pray over as I normally get my local news through the evening TV shows. The USA/Today also has a little section with a blurb from each state, some of which may catch my eye for specific prayer.

The current editorial section on Mondays has been running featured articles about the controversy of religion in today's culture, and it was on this Monday morning that I came across and read the following comment in an editorial response to piety in America and the Golden Rule. It bluntly said:

"How many people do as they please during the week and then put on a show at church on Sundays? This isn't what true Christians do."

I left the paper for someone else to read, but kept hearing the rumbling of this statement in my spirit as I got up to leave. This editorial indictment was like a stake in my heart. Little did I know as I got up from breakfast that the impact of that morning was not over and would increase a hundred-fold.

As I made my way through the restaurant to pay my bill, I walked passed a table where a man was feeding his paralyzed wife her breakfast from his side of the table. I caught myself staring several times as I watched him prepare each spoonful of food and timed it to reach her mouth (her body was shaking), and then watched as he stared at her as she completed swallowing each bite and then waited for the next one.

This is one of those seminal moments that are life changing. I feel like that little picture is what David talks about in Psalm 84:5, when he says, "And how blessed all those in whom you live; whose lives become roads you travel..." (The Message) It was like I was given a moment to read their road, to read part of their journey. I virtually staggered to my car, reeling with both statement from the paper and this picture of living sacrifice. Knowing I was captured by these pictures I also knew I would be processing, praying and journaling these events for days to come.

Now obviously, I don't know if this man was a Christian, but I can tell you it looked and felt a whole lot like Jesus. I also know what these corresponding events made me feel like. I know that I am longing and contending for the church to be redefined on the basis of what we do, or how we live, and not just how we think. We all seem to be waiting for this kind of change, for something that will happen to make today's church more attractive to our culture.

I am not a rocket scientist, but I do know when God has backed me into a corner trapped between truths. The editorial statement in the paper and the picture of the raw practical love between this couple had gotten my attention. I was undone. And it was a set up linked to another article called the Attractional Church that someone had sent me a few months ago.

In the article it stated that the early church experienced significant continual growth even during the decades of persecution, and gave the reasons why.

"And yet the early church grew and grew and grew, even without intentional evangelistic strategy or ministry. How? By being the most attractive community in the Roman Empire. The early Christians rescued abandoned babies and raised them as their own. They gave burials to all, regardless of economic status. They cared for the sick and dying, even if that meant their own deaths. It was said of the early Christians "they alone know the right way to live. It wasn't until after Constantine that conversion became a matter of advantage rather than attraction, or eventually by compulsion. Only after Constantine did people reject the church on moral and ethical grounds and begin to accuse Christians of hypocrisy. Prior to that, the church was known as the people of compassion, love and peace. It was interesting to ponder how the church could recover that kind of pre-Constantinian attractiveness in our post-Constantinian, post-Christian, postmodern context. For those of us who have struggled with being "evangelistic," it's encouraging to know that the early church grew not because they were distributing gospel tracts but because they were practicing hospitality, neighborliness and social concern for the poor and marginalized. That still seems to me to be a prophetic counterculture stance in today's context."

Somehow our preoccupation with our belief systems, our meetings, our programs and everything it takes to protect them has actually made us almost invisible to our world and how to impact it.

I remember when we had our first Unconference with Graham Cooke in San Diego several years ago. A local newspaper showed up to write an article about Graham and Third Day Churches. They quoted him as saying.

"The church in the west is living in some sort of bizarre alternative universe. A large part of the evangelical church is Pharisaical. The church is set up to keep people in place," said Cooke as he reclined on a couch. Cooke believes the church is what keeps people from God." The church is missing it. What we are doing is largely irrelevant to a whole bunch of people." Cooke suggested that God may not answer people's prayers for revival because God doesn't want to birth new Christians into the current church." Cooke said (as we have heard him say many times) that the church must move from a "functional paradigm," based on business and systems, to a "relational paradigm."

25 years ago plus, anthropologist Paul Hiebert proposed a better way of understanding social groupings. He divided people and how they connect into three possible groups: centered sets, bounded sets, and fuzzy sets. Years later I would listen to John Wimber refer to these sets in trying to explain what he thought the Vineyard Movement was to be.

Bounded Set: This type of categorization emphasizes essential characteristics and uniformity of the characteristics while maintaining a clear boundary separating what is and is not part of the category. Also, the essential characteristics are static, not subject to change. A piece of fruit, for example, must in substance and shape be like every other piece of fruit belonging to the same category; it is or is not a particular kind of fruit, and it will always be the kind of fruit it is until it is consumed or decomposed.

Centered Set: This type of categorization emphasizes defining the center and how things relate to the center (either moving toward or moving away), that things are not uniform as some are closer to the center than others, and that the boundary is not so clear because the main factor is the center and the relationship of the things to it. An example, Hiebert suggests, is a magnetic field: all the particles are in constant motion, but the electrons move toward the positive magnetic pole whereas the protons move toward the negative pole.

Fuzzy Set: This type of categorization emphasizes how things relate to a reference point (or a number of different reference points representing different categories), making the boundary fuzzy. An "either-or" dichotomy is not characteristic of this categorization. A thing may be partly, halfway, or 88% inside a particular set. For instance, a person's race could be an indiscernible mix of Latino, Quiche and African.

These metaphors are pretty atypical of most of the church groups or church life we have all known. In our church world there are bounded sets that tend to be rigid, legalistic and hard to penetrate or get in. There are also those fuzzy set churches who are soft, sometimes liberal, and even considered loose with little convictions or standards. And then there are those centered set churches or groups that have a softer edge than the bounded sets, but usually function from a clearer and more deliberate center or core, unlike the fuzzy sets.

Len Hjalmarson goes on to say www.nextreformation.com, that it is not that bounded sets are always bad and centered sets are always good. Boundaries do exist. Salvation is a bounded set. One is either in Christ, or not in Christ. Discipleship is a centered set. To be a disciple is to be constantly moving toward the center, which is Christ.

But if we use the centered verses bounded set model, our understanding of what is the center must be very clear. For example from the central teaching of the Kingdom of God in the New Testament the church is not that center, the center is Jesus: the Head of the body. All members of the body are to function in relation to the center: Christ.

It has been said that generally our theology is sound, but our practice is not. In fact, most evangelical churches are orthodox in belief, but heretical in practice. So what is it about us that we say we believe in Jesus but we do not love and impact our world as He did?

The boundary markers for the church must be determined by where the gifts and callings of God's people take them, rather than an artificial standard. If believers were encouraged and enabled to seize the opportunities God brings their way in the neighborhood and across society, and if they could proceed confident of support from others in the body, the church would be redefined.

And this shift in how we think as the church would most likely cause a change from us being a bounded set to becoming more of a centered set modality.

I guess my point is this. We can spend all of our time polishing the walls of our bounded set systems, making sure we are precise in our doctrines, dotting our i's and crossing our t's, keeping anyone out who may not totally agree with us. Or we get so sloppy and so culturally relevant that we actually have nothing to offer the world because we have become the world. Or, we center in on Jesus and who He is, and what He wants to be released to do through us to make a difference in our world and become centered-set, or centered-strong in Him.

If we really submit to the Jesus style of 24/7 radical discipleship and mission, it will be less about our meetings, less about our apologetics, less about our sermons, less about us building stronger walls to keep our bounded sets bounded and secure and more about living daily with passion filled lives in a broken world, with Jesus at the heart of it all.

It will be more like that loving husband feeding his handicapped wife.

It will be more about venturing outside of our bounded set, Christian fortresses with our ninety-minute inspirational weekend meetings and recklessly joining in the exploits of God in a desperate world. It could mean dropping our doctrinal differences and walking hand in hand with other brothers and sisters into the streets of our cities, making a real impact by seeing what God sees and responding as He responds.

It could mean that even in the 21st century we might choose to be like that "attractional church" that actually threatened the status quo of Roman Empire by its actions and not just its artsy articulation.

I am tired of my Sunday or weekend performances; I want to touch my world and impact it for God. I don't want to be so doctrinally driven that I must spend all of my time and energy polishing the book and protecting my club through a stiff functional paradigm.

I want to be so relational with God and others that my life overflows with outrageous and contagious love and affects everyone around me. Maybe they could say in the old film, "Field of Dreams," "Build it and they will come." But that doesn't work anymore. You can build the finest cathedral in town, create the most vibrant ministry with the cleanest infrastructure and that doesn't mean it is attractive to the lost.

Our buildings and programs don't attract. Our belief systems and our precise teachings don't attract. It is our lives filled with unbounding love and sacrifice. It is not just what we believe but how what we believe impacts the way we live. I don't want to be ignored anymore as I simply try to survive in my Christian ghetto. I want to turn my world upside down.

This time we get to "be" the message. Be giving, be kind, be sincere, be patient, be caring, be generous, be forgiving, be impartial, behonest, be understanding, be outrageous, and "be" Jesus to our world and then they will have cause to ask us why we are the way we are.

"Evan Almighty"

In the last scene of the current movie about a modern Noah, called "Evan Almighty," God (played by Morgan Freeman) smiles, laughs and dances. That is the kind of Attractional Church I want to be a part of.

The Challenge of the New Church

There is an old story about five blind men who were given the task of describing an elephant. Depending on where the men were positioned, they in turn described the elephant as a mountain, a fire hose, a tree trunk and a spear. (The blind man who grabbed the elephant's tail and thought it was like a fly-swatter had the presence of mind to keep his mouth shut.) The story doesn't go into detail about the fighting that took place between the other four to resolve the issue, as apparently none of them considered that they could all be partially correct.

God is infinitely more complex than the elephant. Many of us have had an experience with God that has given us a certain impression of what He is like. However, God is just too big for us to experience more than just a small part of Him. Many people live their entire lives being satisfied with their partial view of God, either by choice or out of ignorance that there is perhaps more to see. Others learn to relate to others who have a different experience of God, and hopefully increase in their knowledge of Him in the process. However, we don't increase in our experience of God by merely relating to other Christians. To do that, we must occasionally reposition ourselves, stepping out of the box of our personal traditions, so that we can experience God from new angles.

It has been my intent over the few years to keep "walking around the elephant" and to take as many others with me as I can drag. As a result, it was often hard to describe our various home groups, as we rarely did things the same way twice. We had, as our primary values, relating to God, and relating to each other, and found that these values could take on many forms. I often found that it was the group who was dragging me around to some new view.

However, working within the structure of a church, even a smallish church, has proven to be more difficult. There seems to be an innate rigidity in the typical church that resists attempts to do something new, or merely to do something in a new way. No matter how much we talk about valuing organism over organization, it seems as though where two or more or gathered, the system (or "the machine," as we say) takes over.

Of course, everyone resists change to some extent. The fact that we were created with skeletal systems indicates that we are creatures who depend upon a certain amount of structure. People groups also require a certain amount of structure. Put 50 people together and they will in very short order create some kind of functional system, whether it's just to decide who will go get the chips and beer. But, take 50 people, or even 10 people, and have them start a "church," and superfluous structures begin forming out of thin air - or rather, out of our notions about what a church should be. The concept of traditional church has a power that is almost impossible to withstand.

I think this has a lot to do with the cultural expectations of "church," which unfortunately seem to have become the Western church's secondary cornerstones. A few years ago I sat in a room with about 12 people as we considered how to start a new church. The question before us was, "what are the essential elements of a church?" I was astounded at many of the responses, and by the extraneous work that people were willing to take on (which, by the way, took time and energy away from developing community). Things like the Sunday Morning Service and the Head Pastor model, though neither has any real New Testament basis, have actually become foundational to our concept of church.

Let's take another look at our blind men. Each one, being fairly happy with their position at the elephant, starts laying a few stones. The first one, the Head Pastor stone, marks one corner, directly across from the cornerstone marked "Jesus." The next stone, the Sunday Morning Service stone, marks another corner, and so on. Pretty soon the foundation is laid and the church is built, and there it will stay, with no means of ever discovering what lays outside the box they now call the church.

So how do we do church differently? How can we create a structure that does not prevent us from discovering the many facets of God? What we need is something that moves - we don't need a monument, we need a hovercraft!

The first thing we need to do is realize that the aforementioned cornerstones are not cornerstones at all; we cannot afford to entrench them. They may be useful tools for some churches at some times, but they are not essential to being the church. The only essential elements of church that I can see are contained in this statement: "wherever two or more are gathered in my name, there am I in the midst of them." That is church, pure and simple. Relying too much on anything else creates immobility and contributes to an "us and them" mentality within the church (something that Paul warned against in 1 Corinthians 3:4).

We also need to establish among our people the value of remaining fluid. However, in order to do that we need to provide some new, transportable base upon which to build this fluid structure. We already have, of course, our only real foundation, which is the Gospel of the Kingdom. To this we add no other foundation; we only add the "architectural guidelines," if you will, for our structure.

My current thinking (my thinking is pretty fluid, too) is that all we really need besides the Gospel is inherent in the Gospel itself, which can pretty well be described by the intertwined concepts of "relationship" and "community." The Gospel is only lived out as we are first in relationship to the Head, Jesus, to the rest of the Body, the Church, and of course in relationship to the world. Again, we come back to Jesus' statement, "wherever two or more are gathered in My name, there am I in the midst of them."

So, then, we have the foundational rock of the Gospel, which of course, rests solely on the work of Jesus. That, in effect, is our "elephant." To be a church, I think we should be in relationship with the entire elephant, not just the part we think we know, or like, or what fits our personality. At least, we should be willing to be in relationship with the entire elephant, though we know that is impossible considering our human limitations. This means we must have, as one of our highest priorities or values, a commitment to being fluid enough to be in relationship with all of God. This, of course, presupposes a belief that we, ourselves, are myopic in our view of God and of the Church, as well as in our view of ourselves.

Next, we must be committed to each other. Throughout our journey we will, hopefully, bump into various other like-minded people and "clump" together (the fellowship that Todd Hunter has been working with calls itself "a fearless clump of seekers"). We will also hopefully "convert" others along the way, who will also clump with us. This is a natural, organic development of church. In my opinion, this is The Way It Should Be. We need to have as a co-equal value, a commitment to those that God has clumped together.

This commitment includes allowing our interaction to lead us in new understandings of God. Not valuing the "head pastor" as essential, we will probably not have just one person navigating the way; the direction of our journey will be set as we interact as a group with God.

A third value (actually, it's part B of our 2nd value) needs to be a commitment to the rest of The Church. Again, we cannot afford to have an "us & them" mentality. In our fellowship's journey together around the elephant (we are no longer a blind man, we have become a visionary fellowship), we will encounter both other visionary fellowships as well as the structures built by our blind men. They each have an experience with God that is also part of us; for in reality we are the same body. As John Donne once said, "no man is an island." The same holds for fellowships. We are part and parcel with each and every visionary group and blind man who has a relationship with God, and we must value that to the same extent that we value relationship within our little fellowship clump.

Of course, we need to realize that most of the blind men, as well as many of the other visionary groups, may not hold to this value, and may despise what they perceive as our lack of foundation. No matter - we must continue to value them, and to look at their position to search out any truth that we may need to discover.

What else do we need? Oh yes, a good Sunday School program. OK, so I am just kidding. I don't think we really require anything else. Everything else - missionary sending, outreach, Bible study - all will come naturally if we are truly and honestly relating to God and are sensitive to His leading. My theory is that our commitment to being fluid and walking around the elephant will make our fellowship more apt to follow the leading of the Spirit. When the woman at the well tried to engage Jesus with a theological discussion about which mountain God was at, Jesus gave her a remarkably postmodern answer: God is seeking those who will worship Him in Spirit and in Truth. With these commitments - as this really what I have been talking about - everything else should follow.

However, let us state one more relational commitment, which is implied in our commitment to the Gospel: our commitment to the world. Though it is my belief that the church exists primarily to be in relationship with Christ, Jesus came For God So Loved The World. Because it is Jesus' mission to be the mediating savior of the world, our commitment to Him and our relationship with Him joins us securely and permanently to His mission. Though this is the subject for another time, let me just comment that our growing relationship with Jesus only comes as we join Him in going where He goes and working along side of Him.

To quickly summarize, I have boiled the essence of church down to a commitment to three relationships: 1) A vital, growing and changing relationship to God, 2a) A relationship to those we "clump" to, 2b) A relationship to the entire Church, and 3) A missional relationship to the world. These commitments will require some type of structure; don't misunderstand me as saying that all structure is wrong. I am just challenging us to rethink our structures, as I suspect that we can find newer, more efficient and more relevant structures.

As I have dialogued with people over the years about the lack of need for so much rigid structure in church organizations, usually referring to my home group as a model for how church could work, often there has come the argument that this can only work for a small group. Once a church reaches a certain size, they say - say 100, 200 people - you can't do church the same way; then you need to move into a more conventional structure.

I honestly don't know if that theory is true. Perhaps at a certain size, even with commitment to the values I have mentioned, fluidity is hampered. If so, then, it begs the question, "why do we need churches that big?" It sounds to me that once size is a problem, operating in smaller groups would be a solution, which is basic cell-church theory. The difference here, however, is that cell-churches have often fallen into the blind man category as they have entrenched themselves in their own positions.

I am not suggesting that the New Church cannot meet on Sunday mornings, or that they cannot have a single or head pastor. They can even own a building with a steeple, if they feel led, just as long as they don't make it foundational to who they are, or insist that others do it, too. The New Church needs an attitude of humility and a commitment to flexibility, founded upon the principle that "we know in part," that we need to know more [of God], and that we will do anything we need to do to know Him more fully and to communicate to the world.

That is the challenge facing The New Church.

The Church Service Community

Mary, Mary, quite contrary How does your garden grow? With silver bells and cockle shells And pretty maids all in a row.

For the past generation, one of the hottest topics among pastors and church leaders has been church growth. "Pastor, Pastor, quite contrary, how does your garden grow?" Theories abound and models for 'doing church' come and go like teenage fashion fads. But in the middle of all this discussion and strategy a few very practical questions remain: "How does God intend his church to grow? What are the means by which the gospel of Jesus is spread? What is the job of the average Christian? How should pastors lead in this endeavor?" One attempt to answer these questions should be very familiar. For lack of a better name, I will call it the 'Church Growth' paradigm. Here are a few of this paradigm's basic assumptions:

A simple vision - bring the gospel of salvation in Jesus to the entire world by any means necessary.

Ethnic groups - generational groups, special needs groups, etc. are identified, studied, targeted, and advanced upon with this gospel in hopes that they will be assimilated into the Kingdom and a church.

Massive amounts of funding - personnel, strategy, planning, and leadership are necessary to pull off this enormous undertaking.

One of Church Growth's primary tools is to coax people into a special place once a week where God is the focus of the entire event (traditionally, a service on Sunday morning). The idea is that if people will think about God for a few hours on Sunday, maybe they'll also consider him the other 166 hours during the week. All manner of resources are expended to make those few precious hours as efficient and relevant as possible. Countless programs are concocted to try and connect people with God at other times. The amount of blood, sweat, prayer, and tears expended in this paradigm is extraordinary.

As a reward for all that effort, Church Growth has been extremely successful. The gospel has reached more corners of the world than ever thought possible in the last 100 years. But without going into the problems associated with Church Growth, let me propose another way to answer those fundamental questions. Let's assume that you've tried Church Growth and found it wanting. Or, you've simply run out of silver bells and cockle shells and pretty maids all in a row. This next paradigm I would like to describe is much less popular and remains largely untried in North America. Again, for lack of a better name, I will call it the 'Subversive Community'.

'Subversive' is an odd word to associate with Christian ministry, but that is only because of its uses in recent world history. Webster's defines 'subvert', "to overturn or overthrow from the foundation." It's origin is Latin, "subvertere, literally, to turn from beneath." Eugene Peterson has a great description of this paradigm's assumptions:

"Three things are implicit in subversion. One, the status quo is wrong and must be overthrown if the world is going to be livable. It is so deeply wrong that repair work is futile. The world is, in the word insurance agents use to designate our wrecked cars, totaled.

Two, there is another world aborning that is livable. Its reality is no chimera (illusion). It is in existence, though not visible. Its character is known. The subversive does not operate out of a utopian dream but out of a conviction of the nature of the real world.

Three, the usual means by which one kingdom is thrown out and another put in its place - military force or democratic elections - are not available. If we have neither a preponderance of power nor a majority of votes, we begin searching for other ways to effect change. We discover the methods of subversion. We find and welcome allies."

The Subversive Community's mission is not to bring the kingdom of God from without; it is to release the kingdom of God from within. Subversives do not "reach outside people and encourage them to come in." Subversives live and do their work 'undercover' where the world lives and breathes. Their goal is not escapism (trying to build a Christian utopia), but to show people how they can lay hold of life as God intended, in his Kingdom.

The Subversive Community understands that the world and its ways are false. It is constantly interacting with people at work, in the grocery store, or at home who are all in the prison of this world's system. These prisoners are quite happy in their assumed reality (especially the ones who have amassed quite a kingdom of wealth). But some secretly ask the question, "Is this really all there is to life?" The Subversive Community's answer is not merely to inform them about the Kingdom, but to invite them to become participants in a whole new reality. The training program will be unique and cannot be rushed or broken down into a few 'principles' that are easy to swallow. Remember, the kingdom of God deals with every aspect of our lives. This training might just take a lifetime.

The chief aim of the Subversive Community is to train other subversives, which is really what the Great Commission was all about. So what are our tools? Where do we begin in this training? How do we train others? Again I'll reference Peterson from "The Contemplative Pastor":

"Prayer and parable are the stock-in-trade tools of the subversive pastor. The quiet (or noisy) closet life of prayer enters into partnership with the Spirit that strives still with every human heart, a wrestling match in holiness. And parables are the consciousness-altering words that slip past falsifying platitude and invade the human spirit with Christ-truth."

Andrew Jones used to have on his website this tag line: "One who tells stories and throws parties." Combine that statement with Peterson's and you get the closest thing to a strategy for church planting available. I call it the "Three-P's of Church Planting" – Prayer, Parables, and Parties.

In the absence of building programs, 45-minute sermons three times a week, and an "outreach ministry," there is prayer. The "wrestling match" to which Peterson refers is not the hand-wringing sessions most prayer meetings resemble. "Oh God, our culture is so bad. Why are people not coming to our church service anymore? Please bless our next outreach program so we can advance your kingdom." Instead of asking God to bless our programs, we should be trying to bless His. This takes a willingness to do two things: ask and wait. Our community has grown through having times of prayer that include more silence than prayer. We are trying to learn corporately the ancient (and anti-Western) discipline of solitude and silence. As we've grown in our ability to hear God's voice, we've found a few simple prayers that have been helpful:

"God, what have you created us to be in our community?" "How can we represent your Kingdom in our jobs, families, circles of friends, and neighborhoods?"

"Make us aware of your rule and reign today in every situation."

"Lead us to men and women of peace that will provide contact with the world in places where your Spirit is working." (See Luke 10)

The Subversive Community is a living story. It sees itself as a footnote to Chapter Three in the Story of God and His People. Simultaneously we are living within the Larger Story, the story of our faith community, and our individual stories. This has always been so, but the church has kept these stories stored away on a dusty shelf and tried to give the world the Cliff Notes instead. It's time to take the musty books down and learn the art of storytelling again.

Jesus understood the deeply subversive nature of stories. He used parables like ticking time bombs of truth implanted in his hearer's minds. They would sit there unprotected, challenging assumptions and coaxing the soul to establish a new foundation for life. N.T. Wright explains:

"When Jesus announced the kingdom, the stories he told functioned like dramatic plays in search of actors. His hearers were invited to audition for parts in the kingdom. They had been eager for God's drama to be staged and were waiting to find out what they would have to do when he did so. Now they were to discover. They were to become kingdom-people themselves."

The Subversive Community can use parable in many different ways. Our community has utilized the Web to tell our story on a global and local stage. The recent web-logging craze (www.blogger.com) has enabled us to keep our story documented real-time and from the point of view of each participant. Music, art, and poetry allow the community to present the story in fresh, creative ways. Even something benign like how you design your house can communicate truth about the Kingdom. Parable is in its nature a creative act so it is most effective when you decide to be original and invite the Holy Spirit to tell God's story through your life. Don't just use someone else's stories; come up with your own!

"People will come from east and west and north and south, and will take their places at the feast in the kingdom of God." (Luke 13:29) Jesus often used the party or feast to represent the kingdom of God. His first miracle was performed at a wedding reception, he feasted with his brand new followers Levi and Zacchaeus, and his most famous parable ended with a huge party for a prodigal son. Often, Christians think true spirituality looks more like fasting than it does feasting. But Jesus responds, "Do wedding guests fast while celebrating with the groom?" (Luke 5:34) The Subversive Community knows how to party.

Our community has organized a few parties, which we call Kingdom Feasts. We invite friends, family, co-workers, people from other churches, and anyone else who wants to come. The last one was held at the beach where we cooked a ton of burgers and played volleyball in perfect South Florida weather. Another time we fried up a bunch of shrimp and worshipped into the night. But each time, our focus as participants is to demonstrate to ourselves and our guests that the kingdom of God is here.

The Subversive Community would never be caught trying to coax the world into a church building. It believes the church (which is you and me) exists primarily out in the world just being itself. But we are not passive observers of a world going to hell. We are here to overthrow the world's assumptions about life and our hope for the future. Peterson now completes our job description:

"This is our primary work in the real world. But we need continual convincing. The people whom we are praying and among whom we are telling parables are seduced into supposing that their money and ambition are making the world turn on its axis. There are so many of them and so few of us, making it difficult to maintain our convictions. It is easy to be seduced along with them.

Words are the real work. Prayer words with God, parable words with men and women. The behind-the-scenes work of creativity by word and sacrament, by parable and prayer, subverts the seduced world. The pastor's real work is what Ivan Illich calls "shadow work" - the work nobody gets paid for and few notice but that makes a world of salvation: meaning and value and purpose, a world of love and hope and faith - in short, the kingdom of God."

War Over Wineskins

What does it really mean to **"do"** church differently?
What does **"change"** really mean?
What does **"new"** really mean?

Four Possibilities From New From Roget's II: The New Thesaurus The Editors of the American Heritage® Dictionary.

Main Entry: **new** Part of Speech: adjective Definition: Not the same as what was previously known or done. Synonyms: different, fresh, innovative, inventive, newfangled, novel, original, unfamiliar

Main Entry: **additional** Part of Speech: adjective Definition: Being an addition. Synonyms: added, extra, fresh, further, more, other, new

Main Entry: **fresh** Part of Speech: adjective Definition: Not previously used. Synonyms: brand-new, new

Main Entry: **present** Part of Speech: adjective Definition: In existence now. Synonyms: contemporary, current, existent, existing, now, present-day, new

It seems easy to remain vague about change, until it is defined. With "change" being one of the driving themes of this current election in the US, everyone is crying out for more clarity, more specificity, more steps, more exact actions.

What do we mean by change?
And what are we actually changing?

To see true change come to the church sounds similar to the nebulous political jargon of today. We don't want to offend anyone in the church so we often couch our nomenclature in ambiguous terms, or at least religious ones, like, we just need "renewal," we just need "revival," we just need "reformation."

But without specificity most people read that as we just need a new "program," we just need a new "vision," we just need a new "pastor," or at least newer "buildings," and new, softer "pews."

So, we find ourselves adjusting the lighting, laying down new carpet. Trading in the old pews for theater seats, buying the hottest new flesh tone wireless microphones, firing an old preacher, hiring a new preacher. We work at doing fresh demographic studies and change the order of service.

But this time, that will not be enough, it will not work. All of this is merely patching the wineskins.

Patching the Wineskins!
Patching the Wineskins!
Patching the Wineskins!

So we paint the wineskin, put new carpet in the wineskin, rearrange the seating in the wineskin. Add a second wineskin, maybe even a Saturday night wineskin for the younger set.

Of course none of these changes make a difference over the long haul. Sure, we may get a few kudos about some of the subtle shifts and slight changes we have engineered. But has anything really changed in the long run? We even brag about the changes we have made at the Annual Wineskin Convention, maybe even write a book about our new wineskin, and start an association around this new way of wineskins.

But honestly nothing really changes, all we do is end up diluted the wine, forgetting that the purpose of the church is to accommodate what God is doing, not praying and make God cooperate with what we are doing.

With time these aesthetic adjustments too will fade; this time we need something more. We need a completely "new" way of doing church, a "new" way of being the church: a new way, not an additional way, or even just a fresh way, and definitely not the present way.

In fact, everything we currently call church needs to change, not from the outside in, but the inside out, the issues are systemic, and it is broken and needs to be replaced. We need a complete 'paradigm funeral' on how we do church.

All of this requires a complete and definitive 'paradigm funeral.' A willingness to start all over with a highly missional, highly participatory band of believers, who regularly care for one another and make themselves readily accessible to the lost by inviting them into their homes for "meatings."

Let's return to simple church and a common meal with a common cup, and not "meetings" with more of the "sit, soak and sour," as some professional does all of the talking.

Let's refuse to sit in silence leaving the meeting with more we simply don't understand and definitely can't apply to our lives.

Let's do 24/7 missional church rather than another weekend when we drive to a campus, struggle through a twenty minute search for a parking space, an athletic sprint to drop of the children at the Christian babysitters, another mad dash to the coffee kiosk, and then a press to find a decent seat before the performance begins. Only to look around for the first twenty minutes trying to find the family you want to go to lunch and spend the afternoon with after the meeting.

"Nor do people put new wine into old wineskins, or else the wineskins will break, the wine is spilled, and the wineskins are ruined. But they put new wine in new wineskins, and both are preserved." (Matthew 9:17)

No more crying over spilled wine. Enough is enough, it is now time for a "new" way of doing and being church, not a "renewed," or "refreshed," or "repainted," or "redecorated," or a "refurbished," or "re-patched" one.

No more "patching" of the old wineskins, we have already polluted and diluted way too much of the good wine, the old wineskin couldn't handle the radical lifestyle of the next generation, the passionate, missional movement that is in front of us, even the press to the level of intimate, yet expressive worship of the new wine. It is time for a totally new wineskin.

So, where do we start? We must confront the current church system head on.

1. The current church system is designed to produce dependency on the system.

2. The two major obstacles to removing people from dependency of the current church system are the church building and paid professionals. We need to find a way to create a new organizational system that doesn't rely on either. Jesus didn't.

3. We need to find a way to redeem people's tithe by removing the obstacles (such as buildings and paid staff) and thus releasing it to missional opportunities.

4. Dependency is ultimately dysfunctional because we're not designed to be dependent forever. We're designed to become interdependent mature people who can love.

5. We know how to do 500 people really well. But we don't know how to do 12 people really well. Jesus modeled the latter.

6. The primary concern by the current church system for releasing people to become the priesthood

of believers is heresy. Yet heresy exists regardless. Example: We have 30,000 denominations. Some of them are wrong. Jesus left, releasing His Spirit to lead ordinary people. Can we do the same?

7. Exponential growth happened when people participated in what God was already doing.

Are these specific enough challenges for today's church to face? You will have to decide if they are. You also will have to decide what approach to any remedies you are going to risk. If you are really serious about change and not just a repatch of the wineskin, you will have to ask God what He wants you to do and then address what is holding you back.

It could mean completely rethinking your views on the church as it relates to the land (properties, facilities) the learning (training systems, learning dynamics) and the leadership (styles: both old and new) and then address those models you insist on perpetuating that continue to weaken today's legacy church.

O.K. I don't know what everyone is going to do with their buildings and/or their addictions to them, and I am definitely not a real estate agent. But one thing is sure, we must rethink the price and priority we pay for what was once considered, at least in America, our greatest asset.

We are infatuated by our facilities, many times not realizing that the edifice addiction totally and completely impacts how we think and do church in every way.

In a day when church campuses experience bankruptcy (both physically and spiritually) as well foreclosure, we can no longer feed this Constantinian edifice complex that harnesses our souls to the lending brokers of our day and prevents us from fulfilling our mission.

1. Do we give away our buildings to our local civic governments who will turn them into Boys and Girls Clubs? With, perhaps, a clause in the contracts that we have priority use for off times (weekends) for events or celebrations?

2. Do we remodel our facilities to use them every day as feeding and training centers for the uneducated and underdeveloped? And maybe rent them back for our larger celebrations?

3. Do we redevelop and redesign our entire property to be turned into low cost housing for the poor and homeless? Set up ministry offices and ministry bases for those missionary units to live and work among the poor?

4. Whatever we do, we no longer have luxury to treat the church as a piece of real estate, but as a people, a people highly empowered, highly emboldened, and fully released from the excess weight of mortgage and maintenance to fulfill their mission.

We simply can no longer be a people who "go" to a building for "church." We must become the church wherever we "go."

Having long contended for both the "gathered" paradigm of the church as well as the "scattered" paradigm. And long believed you learn more one-on-one, in small groups, in book groups, small accountability groups, even through "webinar-type" interaction on the internet.

And I love those larger parties the Father gets to throw for us where healings, miracles, signs and wonders, prophecy, sending, and all kinds of innovative and creative worship is released can happen.

Sure, these larger meetings need larger places. So when called by God to do them rent the meeting halls, the restaurants, the civic centers, the school auditoriums, and the stadiums. And if the climate supports, move them outside so the whole world can see.

Having just recently participated in a series of larger, open healing meetings, I really do enjoy the fact that we live in a nation that gives us many options on reserving and/or renting existing larger facilities in our communities on an as needed basis for these larger God-parties.

But as long as the people of God keep making their weekly pilgrimage to the "Church Building," that address on the corner of Main Street will remain iconic. The church is a reality, and not an activity or an address.

The Spirit of God is a guide, not a map. And church is the spontaneous intersection of the journeys of all of those who are led by the Spirit. Those moments in time where those journeys meet and it is authentic and real...man, that is church!

People are the church, so I don't ask people anymore, "What church do you go to?" Or, "Where do you go to church?" But rather, if I am curious, I might ask, "Who they are walking with?" or, "Who are you hanging out with these days?" or even, "Who do you enjoy authentic fellowship with?"

No where does Jesus call us to "Go to church." He does say connect often and build each other up whenever you can. Body life is where a local group of people choose to walk together for a bit of the journey by cultivating close friendships and learning how to listen to God together (Wayne Jacobsen).

Buildings don't meet, people do.

Dr. Joseph Umidi, President of Lifeforming Leadership Coaching states it as simple as it gets.

"Jesus defines "success" as the bottom line of whether or not we are making disciples.

Discipleship is almost entirely relational in a combination of small group and one on one culture, outside of church meetings, and especially through the influence of healthy conversations from healthy families around the table.

Until spiritual fathers and mothers are discipled themselves transformationally, they are dependent on programs and methods that are information transactions more than life transfer."

Life transformation or information transactions? It is pretty easy to see that tweaking a meeting in which the genesis of that meeting is and always has been to create a setting where one man teaches all, simple doesn't work anymore, in fact never has, at least in the arena of disciple-making.

We adjust the length of the meeting, the length of the sermon, the mood in the sanctuary, the acoustics of the sound system, the training of the child care workers. We make the coffee stronger, or weaker, we create signs so there are special places for the visitors to park. We make sure the ushers and greeters are perky, and use breath mints.

And when all else fails we offer a new service time and change the name of the church.

Sorry, this time, no cigar! People need transformation and not just a cooler meeting room in which to receive the sound bites of the latest pop-theology. We must be about the business of making disciples, not collecting people and then trading them like the newest fad of trading cards.

Even Bill Hybels of the Willow Creek Association authentically announced that his "seeker-friendly" congregations did not produce transformational change in the lives of its members; meaning they were not discipled. And George Barna's extensive research states we live with a discipleship deficit in the American church.

The local church was never meant to be led by the Lone Pastor, it was meant to be fathered by an Elder, a local person of wisdom and reality.

So one of the first things we do release natural groupings of people who now meet in our poorly stewarded weekend buildings to meet in the places we already have, i.e., houses, apartments, offices, recreation centers, even public sites such as beaches, restaurants, public parks, hotels and pubs.

Yes, these will be much smaller groups, But also far more manageable so a father or mother can lead can lead them transformationally, rather than the masses that gather is our theater style lecture halls each weekend to be stimulated informationally and satisfied intellectually.

When the people of God get unleashed and we actually begin to mobilize masses of people. We create a new synergy for effective leadership, and now no longer require the heavy investment of time, energy and money to in vested Christian CEO mass production in our administrative factories called Bible colleges and seminaries.

And this whole shift? Cheaper, more efficient, and definitely more biblical all the way around.

When the local house churches and smaller ministries get networked into regional movements rather than competitive fortresses, the Elders and the members of the Ephesians 4 team, (Apostles, Prophets, Pastors, Evangelists Who Teach) can circulate "from house to house," or call together larger gatherings for conferences, seminars, workshops, open worship nights, celebrations and parties with lots of sounds, expressions, and participation with the whole body ministering.

We enjoy these larger Christian meetings, celebrations and parties that our culture enjoys, but they are not the life transforming times for intentional discipleship and mutual mentoring that we live in in our weekly smaller groups.

A Pastor (shepherd) is a very necessary part of this whole team. But because he/she cannot fulfill more than just a part of the whole task of "equipping the saints for the ministry," he/she has to be complemented synergistically by the other Ephesians 4 ministries in order to function properly.

A Pastor is a part of that apostolic team, not the sole leader of a local church. That is done by elders who have been released into their vision, their ministry.

Everything starts to look different because it is different, from the top down. People are rightly related to each other now, responsible for their own Christian walk and uniquely placed within a group of people who will help do the rest by mutual, intentional relationship.

The mutual mentoring of these groups led by the Elders, surface any ongoing needs that must be addressed by the Apostolic team, and can either be met by the Apostolic team meeting with the Elders of the house church network in a given area, or even a planned house-to-house rotation of equipping so that everyone gets both nurture and empowerment on a regular basis.

The natural fathers, are in the best place to assess and assist in assimilating the life transforming process no matter how long it takes, or how many tracks it goes down.

This kind of leading and growth does not come through the routine, predictable sermonizing of non-strategic sermons and one endless series of messages. This type of fathering comes from specifically designed truths that deal with real life issues within the lives of the believers in house groups in real time.

The groups now experience the benefit of extended times of chewing and re-chewing in the full application and learning of what is being taught. Very unlike the average Pastor's Reader's Digest generic 45-minute microwave PowerPoint versions meant to be the "one-size-fits-all" diatribe during the weekend meeting.

It is a Christian life we are called to, not a series of Christian meetings. Who are you living your life with, sharing your life with, who helps carry your burdens and you theirs? Who are you growing together with, who knows what is your current process of walking out certain applied truths in your own life, in your family and in your community?

Sorry, we can no longer try to patch a sinking ship with bubble gum or duct tape, we no longer can cure the sickness of today's church with a band aid or some new translation or paraphrase of the text. It requires drastic measures this time.

Whatever we have been doing, whatever we have been perpetuating, and whatever we have been paying for is not working.

We must demand a full refund and must start all over. From a full court biblical advantage, full court biblical worldview and a complete New Testament perspective.

This time we must give the old system a timely burial, a final "adieu," a complete "buh bye." And step up to the bar, as the best wine has been preserved to the last (John 2:9, 10).

This time we have been given permission to do church differently in the 21st century, and with new wineskins.

The City Church

The early church fathers "turned the world upside down" with their witness. They did not have automobiles, telephones, the internet, or airplanes. Yet they successfully planted kingdom colonies in city after city. They had something that God was pleased to bear witness to with supernatural signs and gifts of the Holy Spirit. Since that first generation of pioneers, the world has not been the same!

You can see evidence of their effective strategy in the New Testament epistles written to the churches in the Bible. For example, 1 Corinthians 1:2 says "...to the church of God which is at Corinth...." Ephesians 1:1 reads, "...to the saints who are at Ephesus...." Philippians 1:1 mentions "...the saints in Christ Jesus who are in Philippi...." Col 1:2 is addressed "...to the saints and faithful brethren in Christ who are at Colossae..." Ah, you noticed the Letter to the Galatians? Yes, it references churches- plural. But Galatia was a province, not a city!

In each city there was only one church made up of many house-churches. There was no branding or franchising. When Paul called for the elders of the church at Ephesus, they knew who they were, they knew one another, they knew who they were accountable to, and they came together as one man (Acts 20:17). They were the house-church leaders of the entire city. They were given one new mandate by their apostle (Acts 20:28).

The historic church of the first Apostolic Era had two expressions of corporate life: small groups meeting in homes and the city-wide gathering or network of all the saints. There was no hybrid church like we have today, local congregations. Facility-based congregations are like synagogues in that they have a building devoted to their meetings. Christian congregations as such have been and always will be a blessing. But they do have two major problems: 1) They are too large to meet in private homes. 2) They don't interconnect with the rest of the Body of Christ in the city.

If you add to this dilemma another reality, that modern churches were not founded on the proper foundation of apostles and prophets (Ephesians 2:20), you have another difficulty interjected into the challenge. Most contemporary churches are not answerable to apostles nor do they receive regular input from prophets. They are usually governed by pastors or elders or boards and these usually fight to maintain the status quo.

These early Christian pioneers transformed a fiercely antagonistic Roman Empire that crucified thousands of them and fed hundreds of them to the lions or burned them at the stake. They endured awesome tribulation. Their brave preachers had one basic strategy. Wherever there was a Jewish synagogue that would receive them, they went there first and proclaimed the same Messiah their prophets had foretold in their sacred Scriptures. Then, expelled or persecuted, they would go from house to house among the Gentiles, meeting with groups of new believers in their homes. It was this latter strategy, seemingly accidental-- the development of small house churches throughout each city-- that was the true secret to their phenomenal success.

The only way they could do this was by turning laymen into leaders. They did this in small group settings or sometimes in rented halls. These new leaders could in turn tend to the sheep and could continue to expand the ministry of the gospel without becoming paid professionals or becoming priests in a synagogue performing sacred services for their livelihood. These leaders invaded and conquered their pagan cultures, waging spiritual war while remaining below enemy radar.

These heroes of the faith were nameless, faceless, ordinary men and women, not superstars. But they were outstanding workers. And they were all home group leaders and also members of a apostolic teams. The apostle Paul names many of them in his greetings at the end of some of his letters, folks like Phoebe, Priscilla and Aquilla, Mary, Andronicus and Junia, and others too numerous to mention. The apostolic ministry was not a one-man show but a team constantly qualifying and multiplying new workers. You may have noticed many of them were women. Others were husband and wife. By every measure of success, they succeeded.

God's Performance Evaluation for church leaders today could be, "Are you equipping the saints?" A performance evaluation precedes a promotion. Ask yourself: Are the believers sitting in our congregations discovering their purpose in life, learning the awesome power of prayer, growing in their knowledge of the Lord, and excitedly thwarting the devil's work? Or, are they frustrated, bored, and over-fed?

Admittedly, equipping believers for the work of the ministry is nearly an impossible task given our present church structures and religious expectations. Our meetings are too big, too formal, and too dependent on skilled oratory, amplified music, and polished presentations. Church has become big business. As a result, church staff is usually too busy caring for programs, budgets, and buildings to develop the ministries that God has hidden among the saints. Besides that, making the mental and theological transition from "me fulfilling my ministry" to "helping equip them to fulfill their ministry" is too big a hurdle for many contemporary church leaders to jump over.

I love pastors. But they are too few to get the job done. And often their good past prevents their better future. Most modern pastors are good preachers. They are the product of good seminaries, Bible colleges, and historic denominational church models. They may not realize the standard their Chief Shepherd uses to measure success. Christ uses Ephesians 4:11 as his baseline for evaluating performance. In this Scripture, our Risen Lord says he deliberately gave certain ministries (apostles, prophets, evangelists, pastors and teachers) in order to do one main thing: equip the saints. What ever this means, equipping the saints is apparently their main job description. Note, in this Scripture, it is not to win souls, which is certainly necessary, nor is it to erect buildings, which may not be necessary at all. We know Jesus came to save sinners (1 Timothy 1:15) and we are ordered to participate in prayer for all men to be saved (1 Timothy 2:1-8). Yet Jesus placed the emphasis on more workers (Matthew 9:37-38). With God, the harvest is never an issue.

Soul-winning would be far more effective if the sheep were the ones reproducing. That's multiplication. If the shepherd of the flock is winning all the converts, that's merely addition. Erecting more church buildings may in fact be the greatest hindrance to fulfilling the great commission. It begs for more professionals to run the business, thus leaving out the huge pool of laymen who are indeed qualified by biblical standards (Titus 1:5-9). Buildings formalize our meetings whereas the Body of Christ is a living organism, not an organization. The real church is alive and corporate, the ekklesia. In the Greek language and custom, this word meant "an assembly of called out ones." These Greek citizens, when assembled, had power to legislate local affairs. This is still true today for the saints: they have spiritual authority when coming into agreement in prayer. This also illustrates the truth that the church is not a building on the street corner but a body of people. As Derek Prince said, "There is no way to say in the New Testament Greek language, 'Let's go to church.'" Why? Because the people are the church not the meeting place.

The five ministries named in Ephesians 4:11 were meant to function even in the context of the post-Temple era, after the fall of Judaism in 70 AD. For awhile, the Church was mostly Jewish. Later, starting in Acts 10, it became mostly Gentile. Until the third century after Roman Emperor Constantine, the church was an underground movement without formal houses of worship. It was led by lay people energized by the Holy Spirit but touched at foundations and transitions by apostles and prophets. They went from city to city and from house to house ministering the Word and training more workers. They were (and are) post-resurrection gifts to the Body of Christ, not organizational titles in a religious hierarchy.

Yes, these five titles are ministry offices-- real badges of heaven's authority-- but even more than that, they are job-descriptions for workers set apart for specific missions. These Five-Fold ministry gifts (Greek, doma) are Ascension Gifts by Christ. They are unique in that the man or woman who occupies this office, the person himself, is the gift. The office gifts are distinct from the charismatic gifts (grace-lets) of the Holy Spirit (also called the pneumatikas or spiritual gifts of grace). The Five-Fold persons themselves are gifts given by the ascended Savior to the whole Body of Christ. Therefore, the office-gift is an identity, a role, and a calling based on God's choice with specific power to act received from the Head of the Church not from men. It is not a charismatic anointing that briefly rests upon someone and then quickly departs. What I mean is this: apostles are still apostles even when they are not obviously anointed. The same is true for God's prophets, and for all the Five Fold ministries.

What is the mission of the Five Fold Ministry? It certainly includes The Great Commission. (Matthew 28:18-20) This is the record of Jesus' final orders to the Church. Jesus spoke this commandment to his eleven remaining apostles. Remember, Judas had killed himself, reducing the Twelve to eleven, and Matthias wasn't yet chosen to replace Judas until days later in the upper room (Acts 1:26). Just so you know, the Bible has fourteen apostles mentioned by name before the resurrection of Jesus and fourteen more are identified by name after his resurrection and ascension. Let this startling fact sink in: The Ascended Lord Jesus is still doing what he did then-- recruiting, equipping, and sending forth apostles and prophets to the Church today!

Jesus showed us how to do it when he gathered his original twelve disciples. Yes, he preached to the mixed multitudes, but he also drew aside his devoted followers for special hands-on training. During his earthly ministry, he demonstrated the kingdom of God by driving demons out of suffering people, by healing people of sickness and disease, by raising the dead, and by preaching the good news of the gospel to the poor. He had both good words and good works. But did he stop at preaching?

No... but that's where most of us draw the line. For modern Christians, church is all about preaching and worshipping. Basically, we think good preaching is what the work of the ministry is all about. We tell the pastor, "Great sermon, Preacher!" We never think to say, "Wonderful to hear that you spent all week with those young people desiring to serve God."

Jesus did more than preach. He modeled a small mobile community of faith (at first, a deeply committed team) that displayed the values of his new kingdom. He loved and trained this small band of brothers so they could know God's will. He showed them how to pray persistently, how to stop reacting in sinful ways, and how to stop judging sinners. He forgave others freely right up to the cross. He gave generously to the poor and he gave away everything the Father had given to him. He deployed these raw recruits, these agents of the kingdom, these revolutionaries of a new age, into the same kind of preaching and healing and mentoring work that he had been doing. Then he did something truly amazing... he got out of their way so they could do it themselves in the Holy Spirit's power.

Understanding Jesus' method helps us see the challenges we are now facing. The congregational model of contemporary Christianity brings with it an unquestioned assumption: that is, if we fill the building with hundreds of people and a few people are being saved, we must be successfully doing the work of the ministry.

For many evangelicals, the problem is that they don't know there is a problem. Our small success deceives us. The paradigm of professional clergy in front of laymen as listeners is so pervasive that we don't question it anymore. The perks of success are too powerful to ignore in our church culture so now we have new ministries springing up with a TV mentality and even small churches in poverty-stricken Third World countries that think they can't do church without a PA system. We've made the building and the size of the crowd our status symbol and the validation of our success.

However, even if successful, this paradigm has several problems associated with it. The first problem is that it is unbiblical. The second problem is that it isn't working well enough to get the job done in our lifetime. The third problem is that it robs ordinary believers of the opportunity to do the work of the ministry by keeping it in the hands of paid professionals. The fourth problem is that there aren't enough resources to build enough buildings to gather everyone inside that God wants saved... such as whole cities!

When the Lord looks down from heaven into a major metropolitan area, does he see only Baptist churches? Does he see only Spirit-filled churches? Does he see only churches inside buildings? What does he see? The answer is—he sees the whole church at once, all of it, every flavor and variety and style you can imagine. They are all his people, everyone who names the name of the Lord and has been redeemed by the blood of his Son.

If you're saved, you'd better learn to love your brothers and sisters, even those of different races or liturgies, since we'll all going to spend eternity together! And if you're following the pattern of the apostles and prophets settled in the Bible and affirmed in church history, you'd better start believing in the legitimate church as it really is: congregations plus a myriad of small house groups and the whole network of all the saints in your city.

Bogging Down

There are many continuing reports of the growing revolution towards smaller, house church gatherings in the US church, with many reports yet to come, and many books to be written. Perhaps one of the most compelling insights comes from a national study on house churches recently released by the Barna Organization (www.barnagroup.org). Based upon an evaluation of the levels of satisfaction of those who attend a house church compared with the views of adults who attend a conventional local church, overall, people attending a house church were significantly more likely to be "completely satisfied" with their experience with the house church than those attending a traditional church.

By definition Barna states that a house church is, "a group of believers that meets regularly in a home or place other than a church building. These groups are not part of a typical church; they meet independently, are self-governed and consider themselves to be a complete church on their own... (They are) sometimes known as a house church or simple church, (and are) not associated in any way with a local, congregational type of church."

But as we hear about the increased satisfaction with people's experience of house churches or simple churches, we also need to hear the corrections, and the concerns of how these smaller relational, organic churches can bog down. Even though we are no longer focused on buildings and budgets, these smaller house church gatherings are not a panacea to all community problems, and in fact, can have their own set of difficulties.

Much of it comes down to a willingness to change what happens when we actually gather, and the ways we live out our faith with each other, rather than a mere fixation on a change of address or some new size of the gathering. After all, moving from one building topped by a steeple to one topped by a chimney is not enough.

To navigate this ever-changing, ever-shifting way of "doing church" requires a decision to be radically relational and different with each other. And it is in the crucible of these smaller, relational church gatherings that some of these new attitudes of relating get flushed out and can get fixed. If we don't change the way we are in these relationships, even these wonderful, smaller, organic-type meetings can bog down.

Henri Nouwen, with his unique relational writings, suggests that intentional, authentic community requires some hard work. To begin with, in authentic community we must be reminded that each person - no matter what religion, race, age, sexual orientation, handicap, woundedness, or creed - is the beloved of God. This universal vision of the human person offers grounding for a peaceful, lively, and creative relationship with all people. The greatest need in the church is best challenged and thus best responded to when the group is small enough so that you are forced to know one another and to choose to learn to love one another.

We went through a very interesting season in the 1980's and 1990's of doing everything we could to attract people to our traditional church gatherings. The whole seeker-sensitive movement taught us that people need to feel loved and accepted before they will ever be open to the message of the gospel. The attractional church set out to create a new atmosphere where broken people could feel genuinely cared for.

At least that was the goal. Parking slots for the visitors to park near the entrance of the facilities, brightly printed bulletins, power-point presentations on large screens, coffee, muffins and an entire team of perky, upbeat greeters. All of this to make the church gatherings feel more user-friendly and more inclusive.

The question is, how much can you really love someone if you don't know them? And don't they know that? Like the old saying, "God is a true friend, because He knows all about you and loves you anyway." Maybe creative, welcoming meetings in an attractional church setting was a positive beginning on sharing God's love with someone. But nothing seems to say, "I love you," more than when your own brokenness is known and yet you are still loved.

Maybe church has its biggest test here. If we want to convey the Father's heart toward each other, it will come across because we will feel both fully known and fully loved. And I don't think this can happen adequately in the typical look-at-the-back-of-the-head meetings we have in our larger lecture halls.

Even with the best team of greeters you can train, a warm handshake, or even a good strong hug; will not take the place of spending face-time with each other, getting to know each other and getting to really love each other. When anything gets in the ways of this growing in love, church bogs down.

It has been my privilege for over a dozen years to sit along the boardwalk in Pacific Beach (San Diego, California), listening to my unique friends and observing what I have come to call "the parade of parenting." Because kids come in all sizes, all shapes, all conditions, all circumstances, it has been quite a parade. Parents rollerblading with younger kids, biking with older kids, parents skateboarding that should not be. And then there are those special moments of moms and dads pushing children in wheelchairs, or simply walking along with them holding their feeble hands. It takes all kinds of love for all kinds of kids. This too, is the church on parade. When we don't deeply, consistently and intentional love, church bogs down.

In intentional, authentic community every person experiences fear, doubt, insecurity, and brokenness. When we acknowledge our vulnerabilities and discover in them new strengths, we also find ourselves empowered to love and serve others. Community is where the integration of our strengths and weaknesses becomes a sign of hope to the world.

Given the fact that we have all known the risks of transparency and openness in small groups, a growing honesty still must be restored to grow in community. The whole concept of true fellowship is people walking in proximity with a "lighted" path, (The Epistle of First John).

Openness breeds openness, honesty releases honesty, and hiding always short-circuits true community. When we keep our sharing and openness at the politically correct level of just enough to get by, fellowship really does bog down, and gets stuck at that level.

It almost sounds like a paradox, but Nouwen warns that true, authentic community springs from each member's willingness to spend time alone with God. When we recognize in our solitude that our belovedness is grounded in God, we are not as dependent on others to guarantee our truth or our value as persons. Rather, we become free to give and receive love in response to need rather than in search of acceptance and affirmation. We can learn how to dance creatively between solitude and community.

When I do not maintain the depth of face-time with my Heavenly Poppa in a Sacred Space, I simply will need too much from the group, and need too much from the corporate gathering. This seems to me why so many people continue to be disappointed and continue to vent their frustration about church, as we have known it.

As "God besought lovers," we need to be warned that it is possible to become addicted to certain kinds of corporate meetings that actually compete with the time our Father wants with us personally. Rosalind Rinker once wrote, "prayer is a conversation between two people that love each other." What if our many, high-powered, corporate intercession gatherings actually are in tension with our call to bridal intimacy with the Lord through our alone personal times? Getting together with other believers for corporate worship and intercession is awesome, but not when corporate becomes the enemy of intimate. Following God first and foremost is about 'cultivating the garden of your inner life,' and secondarily feeding a corporate identity.

Christian community it is about people who "know" their God and then come together to build others up in what they "know." Church is not about meeting to get your needs met, but about believers gathering to bring the "surplus" of their life in God to share with each other. It becomes selfish to continue to come to fellowship time after fellowship time with other Christians and maintain that consumer mentality of "what do I get out of this." True community comes out of the wholeness of your alone time with God, and gets bogged down when it is too much about the meetings with others and what you can get from those meetings.

Finally, in taking Henri's lead, authentic community is where we help those who are suffering not merely from a sense of social justice but because we have a deep sense of our interconnectedness with all people. And in the helping, in the giving, in the releasing, and in the being sent to those outside our group, we too are nourished? God is always "missional." He so loved the world that He gave. Jesus was the "sent one," "the Immanuel, God with us."

When we get to know who we are called to walk with, that includes not only the brothers and sisters in our fellowship times, but also the "oikos," or pre-Christian friends, or circle of influence that has strategically been placed in our path. The pathology of what has been described as "koinonitis," where Christians spend too much time "naval gazing" bogs us down. There must be this dance of the gathered and scattered church, the "coming" and "sending," the being "filled," and being "spilled."

This is a season of enormous revelation about how our relationships, our ways of relating to one another can grow. We have all been in meetings where the love seemed tentative, and the criticisms leaked out. We have all been in meetings where the sharing was superficial and calculated. We have all been in meetings where the sucking sound of "meet my need," was too loud because we were living with an underdeveloped personal history with God. And we have all lived way too long with an "us" and "them" mentality towards the harvest.

Let's make a commitment this time to not just change locations from the institutional building to the organic house gathering, but let's grow in being loving, honest, intimate with the Father and missional to the world we live in so today's church doesn't get bogged down.

Why People Gather?

Unwittingly, Third Day Churches has been labeled "just another house church movement." While we do frequently gather in homes (as well as many other places), we are really a permissional movement that looks for God to give us direction as to a variety of ways in which we can and do gather.

We gather as frequently for meetings centered on prayer, mission, and worship as we do the deep fellowship that comes from smaller gatherings of believers centered on meals and mutual edification. And these gatherings take place in homes, apartments, coffee shops, restaurants, on a street corner, in business offices, just about anywhere. It is our goal to gather according to God's strategy and design in a specific way that reflects His nature in the given community, region or locale that we might gather in.

From the very beginning we have tried to pay attention to what we call the dance, or cadence of the people of God. The people scattered (smaller groups) and the people gathered (larger groups). And we have tried to discern the clear set focus or objective of each kind of gathering. And not just gather, but also more importantly "be" the church wherever we are.

Each time we gather, we feel that particular gathering has an optimum dynamic that needs to be embraced. For example, you do not look for intimacy in a large eclectic group, anymore than you look for the dynamic of a larger worship celebration-context is a small intimate group. And if you gathered for prayer you don't necessarily do a lot of outreach, and if you are gathered for equipping or teaching, you don't always do a lot of worship.

While there is a continuum of pursuit of a central objective for God's people gathered, every gathering seems to have a distinctive. The practice in our gatherings that pursues the full potential participation of the priesthood of all believers is tantamount. This really is the ultimate goal of the gathered people of God. Whether for teaching, worship, fellowship, it is the potential full priesthood released that must once again be honored as the people of God gather. We must keep trying to make room for more than just one voice, one view, one angle, one perspective, and one gift.

When we gather, we are asking, "What does the Father want to do?" Many years ago we began asking, "what are the dynamics we are committed to for a given meeting?" Learning from the three dynamics of the "Jethro II Principle," *(Exodus 18:21)* as articulated in the book, "Permission Granted To Do Church Differently in the 21st Century," freed us up to continue to experiment with different meetings for different reasons.

Seeing the church as only a weekend, larger lecture ignores the potential and the health of a group of believers where everyone can participate. For the most part, by Jesus' example, and that of the early church we see the smaller, intimate, platoon of believers following more closely the biblical pattern of mutual-edification.

This still includes practicing and experimenting with designated times for direct, intentional teaching, or equipping, as well as enjoying the love and intimacy of the smaller-sized group. It means enjoying the challenge of the eclectic, interactive variety of the medium-sized group, and also delighting in the volume and vision of the larger-sized group with its apostolic/prophetic emphasis.

To be quite honest though, we need to revisit the very basic question of why do the people of God gather, let alone what they do in these gatherings. Any review of the New Testament gives a real challenge as we try to fit everything we are currently doing into what we hope might be biblical models of biblical meetings.

As we too quickly think of the church in terms of "meetings only," there are indications that gatherings of God's people in Acts and after, showed the essence of a spiritual company, something deeply connected around Christ and each other, and not just a weekly "meeting or two." It appears that connects that small company actually causes or precedes the gathering and what happens in that gathering. Who they are together is the precursor to both why they gather and what they do when the gather.

There are so many more things God has in mind for His 'church,' than simply another sermon by an elite professional in a lecture hall. This habit, this predictable pattern of the holy man, doing the holy things, on the holy day, in the holy place must be given a decent burial. How sad, that a living, working, relating organism of believers has been reduced to just "a collection of fish in an aquarium."

At the very outset Our Lord Himself, while on earth, never even commanded His followers to "organize a church," nor hinted of any model of the church as an ecclesiastical institution. Jesus used the word "church" but three times, referring in each case to the "church" as a spiritual company rather than an ecclesiastical organization, a building or an organized meeting.

In the Acts of the Apostles, containing twenty-eight chapters and one thousand and eight verses, covering a period of thirty years, the word "church" as a Christian organization occurs nineteen times, or once in every fifty-six verses. Again, because "church," is more than a meeting, we must start the definition of what "it is," before we try to decide as to how it gathers.

For years, I have warned my colleagues to not be too quick to mistake "cultural Christianity" for "Biblical Christianity." In Acts when they got together, what they did was very fluid, very serendipitous, often spontaneous, always miraculous *(Acts 2, I Corinthians 14)*, and often the result or outcome of the circumstances in and around that spiritual company, the dynamic of their region, and the reality of their current needs. God's intent is simply not the same as the linear agenda and what must happen next, that we westerners to take our meetings and gatherings.

No matter what you feel or choose as your values and how they get lived out in your spiritual company, so much is still subject to your personal or group or cultural preferences, style, logistics, etc. The "church" is really a child of circumstance that gathers differently all of the time, all over the world.

Why our western gatherings have become so predictable and so boring still surprises me. It has become criminal that these weekend gatherings are always the same, rather than becoming a reflection of the creative God of surprises and suddenlies.

In a recent conversation with a friend who is in a totally different stream than my charismatic, prophetic flow, he unfortunately confirmed to me that even in his historic, evangelical world, everyone basically does the same thing, and most of the times in basically the same way.

Every church it seems, whether evangelical, congregational, confessional, charismatic or emerging has a praise band, uses a power-point projection machine, includes a fill-in-the-blank insert in the bulletin to match the power-point presentation, with all of the gatherings tending to last between one hour and fifteen minutes to an hour and a half.

The only variations maybe some congregational readings, maybe a testimony or two, the coffee or lack thereof, maybe the size or décor of the facilities, whether owned, leased or rented, an of course the ministry times, the altar calls. But pretty much everything else is the same. And of course, that includes the weekly, repetitive use of the one-man-teaches-all-clergy-mandate.

No wonder the next generation is leaving today's predictable meetings by the droves. They desire virtual connection, not calendars and choirs; they want real, authentic relationships not repetitive, boring, no brainer forms or religious habits.

They crave an encounter with a personal, mystical God, not a programmed, yawning get-through-it morning homily, and they deeply desire fellow-travelers who care, rather than paid-professionals, who do their Sunday gig and then disappear out the back door to the waiting vehicle until next week's show.

I enjoyed an interesting chat with a new friend the other day that has a lot of church experience. He said to me that the two most important times around the meeting for him, is before the meeting when he connects with his friends, and then after the meeting when he prays for his friends. Go figure.

I am beginning to wonder if the average pastor has become more a gardener than a farmer? The little garden seems to serve the gardener, whether flowers or vegetables, with a limited use or distribution of the harvest, kind of more of the hobby of gardening for what the gardener gets out of the whole process.

The farmer's goal is different; it is to work hard and long, serving the outcome of the harvest, and its distribution or effects on the masses. The purpose to make disciples and equip others for their ministry is the calling, the challenge, and the commitment that leadership must have. We are to serve the harvest, rather than being served by the harvest.

So, when we gather, we are looking more of a stewardship of an atmosphere, rather than an adherence or a litany or the completion of a timed script. We are encouraging the people of God who gather, to "host the ghost," making room for God, trying to hear and see what the Father wants to do in that specific gathering and how He wants to show up through the whole group and not just the preacher. Constantly being aware as they gather of the significance of mutual edification, and the provoking one another to the deeper things of God, as the spiritual company is constantly growing in God, *(Hebrews 10)*.

I recently asked permission of one of our permission leaders in our network if I could pass along their definition and information of their monthly gathering.

They gather weekly in smaller more intimate expressions around fellowship, prayer, discipleship, outreach, etc., and gather monthly for a different kind of expression. I am excited I get to pass this post along to you. It is a good way of seeing the strength and potential of the gatherings we have been referring to.

It's not to give you another sermon. You've had plenty, and if you need more there are many churches locally to hear great sermons at, much less what's offered online.

It's not for a great show. We don't have a worship leader and a great stage presence with lights and screens and sound gear.

It's not for a great Sunday school program, because we don't have that either. We have a classroom, a simple lesson and a time for the kids to come out and play together.

So why do we "get together" once a month, if it's not to have a "church service"?

The Bible tells us that, *"Whenever you come together. Let all things be done for edification (building up). Let all things be done decently and in order,"* (I Corinthians 14:26-40).

1. "Whenever" means the frequency is up to us - daily, weekly, monthly. 2. All means "all" and that's "all" it means right? SO LET "ALL" THINGS BE DONE. a. Psalms (including: poetry, song, teaching, lamenting, crying, devotion, contemplation) b. Teaching (doesn't have to be a sermon by a pastor; could be a word from a brother or a sister, young or old) c. Tongues d. Revelation e. Interpretation f. Prophecy 3. Let all things (a. through f.) be done DECENTLY (the right way) and IN ORDER (the right time).

I want to ask a question. What were the followers of Jesus called from the time Jesus called His first disciples until *Acts 11:26* where for the first time they were called "Christians" or "little Christ like ones". (Incidentally this is about 10-12 years after the day of Pentecost!)

So what were "they" called for over a decade if not "Christians"? How were the identified as being "different" from the Pharisees and the Sadducees and the religious system the represented? How were they identified as being different from any other sect that was present at the time? What identified them as being different from any pagan religion already present at the time? It was the "way" they lived.

When Jesus came He did not bring a new version of the old. He brought something completely new, altogether a new way of being and living. A new way is what He brought to us and a new way is what He brings us too. He said, "*I Am the Way, the Truth and the Life. No one comes to the Father except through me,*" *(John 14:6)*. Jesus brings to us the Way of God; His very life essence in to our beings, our whole beings, every part. Not certain compartments of our lives, ALL OF IT! Not just the holy parts, all of the parts! Not just the Holy days, all of our days are His now! And all of Him is ours now through Christ Jesus.

I don't know what you call the "way" you're currently experiencing church or doing church or being church. But what I do see that is common among the varying names is the return to the "way" of life that Jesus brought to us and brings us too.

For most this is identified as "simple" church. And yet if you've been involved in this "way" of doing and being you'll find there is nothing simple about it! Simple in method sure, but not insignificant by any means in measure. Sure there isn't as much emphasis on meetings being all showy and flashy, big building and staff budgets, and large programs for certain aspects of church life.

Significant in that you no longer can be passive and complacent about your part of being the church. The level of intentionality alone causes growth towards maturity. Often times if you're not part of "getting er' done" it ain't getting done! And that's ok because instead of having it all done for you, you now are required to be part of the process. And this process now allows for all of you to come forward, to mature; your gift, talents, call, vision, messes, mistakes, faults, etc.

And as we live this life out together we come together once a month to share the course of our lives with one another through; testimonies (what we've experienced), teachings (what we've learned) psalms (what has inspired us), prophecies (what has encouraged us), tongues (what has puzzled us), praises & worship (what has blessed us), interpretation (what we've come to understand), revelation (what we've received from the Holy Spirit).

We come together to continue to share in the "way" of living with, in and through Jesus Christ.

And may we all as we continue to live in the "way" of Jesus encounter, experience and grow in the "truth" and the "life" of God!

Again, as we gather, and by the way, getting together is probably ninety-percent of the Hebrews 10 equation, we look for God to lead and orchestrate these gatherings. We do come with some pre-planning and preparation with ideas and thoughts about these gatherings, but we have learned to hold these planned things loosely, so that the God of the infinite and the God of the intimate and the God of the creative can show up and do His thing.

Important?

It is now obvious (at least to some of us) that "housechurching" is not just a bailout reaction for believers currently discontent or dissatisfied with today's church. House Churches (organic churches, simple churches, marketplace churches, etc.) are not just covert gatherings for malcontents, people who have never had very good social skills and can't get along with the traditional symbols of authority.

Worldwide, housechurching will prove to be one of the most effective and efficient modalities for responding to and obeying the Great Commission in the 21st Century *(Matthew 28, Mark 16, Luke 24, John 20, Acts 1).*

House churches are simply a smaller congregation of no more than 20 people. Anything over that number is "pregnant" and ready to "give birth" to another house church. They are fully functioning churches with a commitment to reaching others not by growing a larger church but by helping create more and more house churches.

House Churches are not just renegade bands of Christians meeting together in some covert fashion in suburban cul-de-sacs. House Churches are completely able to provide everything that the New Testament instructs the Church to provide. They are a place where believers come to know Christ, live out the Word of God in virtual reality, while all the time getting loved on and cared for and thus getting stronger to be able to show others the "good news" of Jesus Christ.

Research has found that there are two types of people being attracted to house churches today. The older participants, largely drawn from the Boomer population, are devout Christians who are seeking a deeper and more intense experience with God and other believers. The other substantial segment is young adults who are interested in faith and spirituality but have little interest in the traditional forms of church. Their quest is largely one of escaping outdated structures and institutions. The stuff that does not work, to find a model that does work.

"Every day they continued to meet together in the Temple courts. They broke bread in their homes, and ate together with glad and? sincere hearts..."(Acts 2:46 NIV)

"You know that I have not hesitated to preach anything that would be helpful to you, but have taught you publicly and from house to house." (Acts 20:20 NIV)

"Greet Priscilla and Aquila...also the church that meets at? their house."(Romans 16:3-5 NIV)

"Give my greetings to the brothers at Laodicea, and to Nympha? and the church in her house."(Colossians 4:15 NIV)

In smaller groups like those found in House Churches there is more effectual life learning, more practical application of the Scriptures in people's lives, and more instilling of a basic passion for evangelism, through shared stories and interaction than is possible in the larger church context.

Ministry is effectively accomplished in House Churches because of the deeper intimacy and community shared by believers. As the local House Church grows in depth through Christians living their lives together, then it gets ready to multiply and enter into expansion growth through the planting of other House Churches.

House Churches are especially well fitted to do some things that is sometimes more difficult for larger churches. They are a better place for hands on leadership training as they model very simple ways of helping to facilitate a group. This is usually done best by observation and participation.

Even though teaching and prophetic ministry happen in House Churches, the main principle of facilitation is for the leader to help encourage an atmosphere of interaction and participation. This can be done by almost anyone. And with the potential of releasing a portion of the group as it grows, or even encouraging new leaders to form new groups, any existing group is an incredible resource for empowering leaders for future groups.

After almost forty years of ministry, and leadership involvement in ten churches, I can honestly say that there are more people today, fully involved, fully committed, and fully empowered to lead and are leading that at any other time in my life and influence.

These House Churches are also able to effectively multiply other churches. While using existing facilities, our homes, apartments, parks, beaches, recreation centers, offices, conference rooms etc., we can plant new House Churches quickly. Believers who are seeking to "add" to the Kingdom of God and build their larger ministries when God actually wants us to allow Him to multiply the Church through us have wasted too much time. And way too much Kingdom finance is being wasted to purchase and lease and maintain facilities that live under poor stewardship because of their high prices and limited use.

As an equipper and a church planter, I am convinced we must both speed up the time it takes to release leaders and exponentially plant churches though the modality of House Churches, organic ministries and relevant businesses. It is crucial. We will never even begin to catch up with the harvest at today's pace of seminary or Bible college grads, or the bogged down venues of leadership training in most church systems.

We must accept the reality of an entirely different process of greenhouse training and harvesting of leaders to be released both quickly and effectively to create church planting movements rather than feed the fixation we have with a building, an address, and the maintenance mentality that feeds the church machine of today.

Forget your preferred style or idea of what it means to "go to church." We are in a crisis mode response to the need for laborers "now" being released in God's vineyard. If even a portion of the prophesied harvest comes, there would not enough room in all of the existing church buildings in the nation to hold the "catch." We can no longer think in real estate terms. We cannot even think that more property, or one more single-cell weekend meeting place will suffice. The harvest is "ripe."

Megachurches can't do it, humongous churches can't do it, and even the newest, slickest denominations can't do it. This time we must create and create quickly; smaller, autonomous, flexible "working nets," or working "networks," of tangible, spontaneous gatherings of believers to help disciple those coming to faith. We can do this best through the life process of having meals together, sharing life's ups and downs, and walking as covenant partners in this Christian walk. Or doing the kingdom with friends.

We must "*buy up the time,*" *(Ephesians 5:16)* and cannot rely on the current methods of church planting. They do not work now, so how can we think they can work then? Ask yourself the hard questions, especially if you are a leader. "How many people are trained and released and empowered and leading because of the way you lead?" These are desperate times; we must shift the "way" we do church, as we at the current pace are not ready to move into God's next shift.

Third Day

Jewish sages, ever since antiquity, have recognized this phenomenon concerning the third day in their scriptures. And they have sought to understand its significance.

Their Talmud and Midrash literature reveals that many of these sages concluded that this scriptural phenomenon reveals a divine principle: God will rescue Israel, or a righteous person, on the third day of some great crisis.

Indeed, that is often the case in the narratives cited above. And Jewish Midrash shows that many rabbis interpreted Hosea 6:2 as a reference to the anticipated resurrection at the end of the age.

But some commentators insist that the Bible's many occurrences of a third day motif, especially those in the Old Testament/Jewish Bible, represent a peculiar phenomenon. Those that scholars generally have regarded as most important are as follows in the "New Revised Standard Version":

• The book of Genesis relates that God called Abraham to take a journey to a certain place and offer his son Isaac there as a burnt sacrifice. The text reports concerning this journey, "On the third day Abraham looked up and saw the place in the distance" where he was supposed to perform this ritual (Genesis 22:4). But just as Abraham drew the knife to slay his son Isaac, who was lying on the altar Abraham had made, God stopped his hand and provided a ram caught in a nearby thicket with which to perform the sacrificial ritual.

• Joseph, as Prime Minister of Egypt, imprisoned his eleven brothers. Then we read, "On the third day

Joseph said to them, 'Do this and you will live'" (Genesis 42:18).

• Moses led the Israelites out of captivity in Egypt to Mount Sinai. Under God's direction Moses then said to the people, "Prepare for the third day because on the third day the LORD will come down on Mount Sinai" to meet with them (Exodus 19.11). This third day motif in mentioned four times in this episode (vv. 11, 16). Jews have regarded this Sinai experience as preeminent in Israel's religious history. And it is thought that repetition in biblical narratives divinely indicates their paramount importance.

• As Joshua prepared the Israelites to take the Promised Land, he said, "Prepare your provisions; for in three days you are to cross over the Jordan" River (Joshua 1:11).

• "On the third day [Jewess Queen] Esther put on her royal robes and stood in the inner court of the king" (Esther 5:1). When she made her request to the king, her husband, it saved all Jews from annihilation throughout the entire Persian Empire. Ever since, Jews have celebrated this story of deliverance by observing their popular Feast of Purim.

• King Hezekiah of Judah was sick unto death. But God said to him through Isaiah the prophet, "I have heard your prayer, I have seen your tears; indeed, I will heal you; on the third day you shall go up to the house of the LORD," that is, the temple at Jerusalem (2 Kings 20:5).

• Hosea the prophet predicted that, seemingly during the future eschaton, a Jewish remnant will say of God, "After two days he will revive us; on the third day he will raise us up, that we may live before him" (Hosea 6:2).

The New Testament also contains several third day motifs. Some of them are about God resurrecting Jesus on the third day following his death. The traditional day of Jesus' crucifixion and death is Friday, called "Good Friday." And the New Testament clearly states that Jesus was resurrected on the following first day of the week, it being early Sunday morning.

By counting Friday as the first day, most Christians believe Jesus was literally resurrected from the dead on the third day. Soon afterwards, the early Jewish Christians also set aside Sunday as their special day of the week to worship in commemoration of their belief that God raised Jesus from the dead on this day of the week.

The New Testament gospels also relate that Jesus had repeatedly predicted privately to his disciples that he would be killed and raised from the dead on the third day. And he sometimes said the same thing to the multitudes, though cryptically.

At least twice he cited the Old Testament story of the prophet Jonah being swallowed by a big fish and being spewed out alive unto dry land as a "sign" (type) of his own impending death and resurrection. He said, "For just as Jonah was three days and three nights in the belly of the sea monster, so for three days and three nights the Son of Man will be in the heart of the earth" (Matthew 12:40).

This saying of Jesus about Jonah has caused confusion for some Bible readers. Surprisingly, the New Testament never states categorically what day of the week Jesus was crucified and died, though it clearly affirms that both events occurred on the same day. Yet some Christians rightfully think that the Roman Catholic tradition that Jesus was crucified and died on Good Friday conflicts with the "three days and three nights" of Jesus' saying about Jonah, as well as with the original account in Jonah 1:17.

Some of these Bible readers have concluded that Jesus died on Thursday (and a few have proposed Wednesday). In fact, it is fairly simple to count backwards from Jesus' resurrection on the first day of the week by the "three days and three nights" of Jonah's prophecy (Jonah 1:17): that is, the night of the first day of the week plus the previous day of the weekly Sabbath constituting the third day/night; the night of the weekly Sabbath plus the previous day of Passover constituting the second day/night; and the night of Passover plus the previous day of the Day of Preparation when the Paschal lambs were slain constituting the first day/night. From this counting it is easy to see that Jesus was crucified on (Sunday/Saturday; Saturday/Friday; Friday/Thursday) Thursday, and more specifically, during the afternoon of the Day of Preparation before the Passover Sabbath began at sunset.

However, some biblical scholars have attempted to solve the artificial dilemma which Roman Catholic tradition poses for the chronology of the week in which Jesus was crucified by explaining that the expression, "three days (and three nights)," represents a Semitic idiom meaning "third day."

This explanation appears to have support in the Bible, as both expressions are used interchangeably in Esther 4:16 and 5:1 and in Matthew 27:63-64. Also, Josephus uses these two expressions synonymously in his Antiquities of the Jews, 7.11,6; 8.8,1-2.

But these explanations leave some doubt as to why a seemingly clear and literal prophetic statement in Jonah 1:17 would have been met by an idiomatical fulfillment in the Gospel accounts. It would seem, rather, that a literal "sign" would require a literal fulfillment; and that an approximate "fulfillment" would not do.

Moreover, Jesus often taught in parables and riddles. Distinguished New Testament scholar Joachim Jeremias acknowledges, as do other scholars, that one of the most difficult sayings of Jesus to comprehend is one that contains a third day motif.

In it Jesus had said, "I am casting out demons and performing cures today and tomorrow, and on the third day I finish my work. Yet today, tomorrow, and the next day I must be on my way" (Luke 13:32-33). Obviously, this particular third day motif cannot refer to his resurrection on the third day, but rather may be an idiomatic way of expressing the notion of "completion."

The Bible contains only one account about Jesus' life between the time of his birth and his public ministry, and it contains a third day motif as well. It is the endearing story about when Jesus' family attended a festival at Jerusalem. Afterwards, they began returning home to Nazareth, located sixty-five miles north in the Galilee. At the end of the first day of their journey they discovered that their twelve-year-old son, Jesus, was absent from their party.

When they went back to Jerusalem, we read, "After three days they found him in the temple, sitting among the teachers, listening to them and asking them questions" (Luke 2:46). So, after they returned to Jerusalem to seek their missing son, Joseph and Mary found the precocious Jesus in the Temple, and in this context the phrase, "after three days," does appear to connote "the third day."

Throughout the history of Christianity, biblical scholars have not written much about this repeated third day motif in the Bible. In recent times, German biblical scholar Karl Lehmann wrote a book that was published in 1969, but only in German, which has two excellent sections devoted to this subject.

Edward Lynn Bode has a chapter about it, entitled "Resurrection on the Third Day and the Empty Tomb," in his book The First Easter Morning: The Gospel Accounts of the Women's Visit to the Tomb of Jesus (1970), pp. 105-26. Harvey K. McArthur has a brief but helpful journal article, entitled "On the Third Day," in New Testament Studies 18 (1971-72), pp. 81-86. And W.L. Craig, an authority on Jesus' resurrection, discusses the subject briefly in his journal article, "The Historicity of the Empty Tomb of Jesus," in New Testament Studies 31 (1985), pp. 42-49. These scholars affirm the Jewish interpretation of these Old Testament third day motifs--that God delivers on the third day of crisis--and they suggest that some of them point to Jesus' resurrection on the third day.

Lay biblical scholar Kermit Zarley, a former PGA Tour professional golfer, has written what may be the first book devoted entirely to a thorough examination of these third day motifs in the Bible. Entitled The Third Day Bible Code (2006), in it he claims that many of the Old Testament narratives that contain a third day motif are types, like Jonah in the fish, which point to Jesus. And he applies a principal to them gleaned from 2 Peter 3:8 (cf. Psalm 90:4), that "with the Lord one day is like a thousand years, and a thousand years are like one day."

For instance, he says many Christians have believed that the Abraham-Isaac saga is a type that depicts God sending Jesus to the cross (p. 124). He then claims that the third day motif of this story forecasts that Jesus would live and be put to death just over 2,000 years later (pp. 128-31). A conservative view of biblical chronology does indeed place this historical event just over 2,000 years prior to Jesus' birth. Concerning the other third day motifs, Zarley offers the provocative interpretation that Jesus' expected second coming will occur during the early part of the third millennium following his departure, between the years 2070 and 2250. The author insists that by applying what he calls the "Thousand Year-Day Principle" of 2 Peter 3:8/Psalm 90:4 to these third day motifs in the Bible, it "serves as a hidden code that unlocks God's timetable for salvation history" (p. xiv), thus the title of his book.

Now that we have entered the third millennium since the birth of Jesus, a church movement called "Third Day Churches" is emerging. It is happenning especially in the U.S. among Charismatics/Pentecostals as well as some Protestants and Independents who identify with the emerging church movement. Although these Third Day Churches derive their name from the combination of Jesus' supposed resurrection on the third day and 2 Peter 3:8 and Psalm 90:4, their emphasis is not on the third day motifs in scripture but a new way in which to live and "do church" as they often put it.

It seems that as we enter into the third millennium since the time Jesus of Nazareth made his mark upon this world, Christians are giving increasing attention to the Bible's repeated third day motif.

Perhaps it can be said that they are finally catching up to the Jewish sages of antiquity in recognizing the importance of this phenomenon in the Old Testament. Christians certainly have more reason to both recognize it and seek to understand its significance, if there is any, since Christianity is based on the foundational belief that Jesus was raised from the dead "on the third day" and not some other day.

Fully Emerge?

I am writing this article to my sisters and brothers in Christ, both leaders and non-leaders, who belong to what has come to be called "the emerging church conversation."

The influence of this conversation has been no less than incredible. So much so, that at least to my mind, it can be better described as a phenomenon. And it is picking up steam with each passing day.

I am a student of church history. My studies have led me to make the following observation: Every phenomenon and movement that has set out to reform or renew the church was born with profound shortcomings and weaknesses. And these shortcomings and weaknesses were never addressed until it was too late for them to be corrected. In my own lifetime, I have seen this to be true for the charismatic movement, the Jesus movement, the third-wave movement, and the house church movement...just to name a few.

Because the emerging church phenomenon is still in its infancy, its shortcomings and weaknesses can be addressed now. As Christians who have grown tired of the modern church, we have a brand new opportunity to change the course of church history. I realize that this may appear to be an outrageous statement. Nonetheless, it is true. We have been given a small window to see a complete overhaul of our Christian faith and to be faithful in honoring the heart of Jesus and the vision of the earliest apostles in our own time. This is why I write today.

The following are themes within the emerging church phenomenon that I wholeheartedly applaud and am thankful for:

1. The emerging church phenomenon is exploring fresh ways to revamp and recontextualize the gospel message to postmodern people. Not only do I applaud this new emphasis, but I shamelessly admit that I have a great deal to glean in this area. Thus, I would like to learn more from those who have plowed further in this field.

2. The emerging church phenomenon has placed a long-awaited emphasis on community and relational faith.

3. The emerging church phenomenon has placed an emphasis on rethinking the modern church...its methods, its programs, its traditions, and its structure.

4. The emerging church phenomenon has placed a new emphasis on the Jesus of the Gospels opposed to the exclusive emphasis on the Jesus of Paul's writings.

5. The emerging church phenomenon has placed a rightful emphasis on the importance of Body functioning.

6. The emerging church phenomenon has placed a new emphasis on the importance of narrative.

7. The emerging church phenomenon has dumped the modern penchant to always be certain in answering every spiritual question under the sun. Instead, it has rested content to embrace mystery and paradox in our God.

8. The emerging church phenomenon has re-ignited a healthy interest in the Christian mystics who emphasized spiritual encounter over against mere academic knowledge of God and the Bible. I am absolutely thrilled to hear "ordinary" Christians, and even leaders talk about these themes openly and unashamedly. All of them point to crucial changes that the Body of Christ desperately needs today. Add to

that, I become nearly euphoric whenever I hear of pastors leaving their entrenched positions to rethink the entire basis for their Christian existence. Such a courageous step is both impressive and worthy of deep respect.

Let me again repeat: We are in a season of church history where we face a small window of time for real and lasting change. A window for revolution in the modern Christian mindset and in the traditional practices of the modern church. A window that Christians 1,000 years from now (should Jesus tarry, of course) can turn their heads back to and behold the beginning of a drastic paradigm shift from an old leaking wineskin to a new wineskin hand-crafted by the Spirit of God.

But note...that window will eventually close. And it will close soon.

The emerging church phenomenon is promising, for it embodies many necessary contributions to a fuller embodiment of Christ and His church. At the same time, the weaknesses of the phenomenon, if not honestly and directly addressed, will reduce it to the status of all past renewal movements. Namely, it will end up spawning a new denomination or "movement" which simply puts a few Band-Aids on the church's ills rather than excavating the root of its problems.

I would now like to list what I find to be the weaknesses of the phenomenon along with some bold questions that I hope will foster serious and open dialogue among leaders in the emerging church. Please note that this list betrays the essence and burden of my own ministry and the vision which drives me. Since I have written on these matters extensively elsewhere, I have cited where one can find these threads more fully unraveled.

By my lights, the weaknesses of the emerging church phenomenon are as follows:

1. The emerging church phenomenon has wonderfully articulated some of the major flaws of the modern church, yet like all of its predecessors, it has failed to identify and take dead aim at one of the chief roots of most of its ills.

I firmly believe that the taproot of most of the problems that plague the church in modernity is the clergy system. To put a finer point on it, Protestant Christians are addicted to the modern pastoral office. The pastor is the all-purpose religious professional in the modern Protestant church, both evangelical and mainline.

Please note that my critique is not an attack on pastors as people. Most pastors in the emerging church are gifted Christians who have a heart for the Lord and a genuine love for His people. It is the modern pastoral office and role that I believe is profoundly flawed, and few of us have ever questioned it.

Let me unpack that a bit. My experience in this country and overseas over the last seventeen years has yielded one immovable conclusion: God's people can engage in high-talk about community life, Body functioning, and Body life, but unless the modern pastoral role is utterly abandoned in a given church, God's people will never be unleashed to function in freedom under the Headship of Jesus Christ. I have had pastors vow to me that they were the exception. However, upon visiting their congregations, it was evident that the people did not know the first thing about functioning as a Body on their own. Neither were they given any practical tools on knowing the Lord intimately and living by His life. The reason is that the flaws of the modern pastoral role are actually built into the role itself.

The pastor, by his mere presence, causes an unhealthy dependence upon himself for ministry, direction, and guidance. Thus, as long as he hangs around delivering sermons, the people in the church to which he belongs will never be fully set free to function on their own in a church meeting setting. Further, the pastoral office typically destroys those who populate it. Jesus Christ never intended for anyone to shoulder that kind of enormous responsibility and power.

In the first-century church, there was no single pastor. The Protestant pastor (which includes the evangelical pastor, the mainline pastor, and the non-denominational pastor) evolved out of the Catholic priesthood. The pastor is essentially a reformed priest, and his role has no root in the original vision and story of the people of God.

In Century One, some of the churches had elders who played a shepherding role. But they did not dominate the ministry of the church, nor was the direction of the church exclusively placed into their hands (as is the case with many elder-led churches today like Presbyterians and the Plymouth Brethren). I believe that we are in desperate need to return to these first principles.

Time and space will not permit me to give historical and pragmatic evidence for the above statements, but I have addressed them elsewhere in great detail. I heartily invite my readers to explore both Scripture and church history for themselves and draw their own conclusions.

Pastors can wax eloquent all day about "facilitating," "mentoring," and "equipping" the saints. But here is the proof of the pudding: Let that pastor leave his congregation on its own without any stated leaders for six months to a year, and he will quickly learn how well he has equipped the church. Will that congregation be able to lead its own songs without a song leader or worship team? Will they be able to have gatherings that are under the Headship of Jesus Christ like the early church did? Will every member of the church be equipped to provide life-giving ministry to one another in those meetings? Will they be able to solve problems and make decisions together as a community?

Perhaps this thought has never occurred to you. But what I have just described is precisely what the church planters of the first century did routinely. They worked themselves out of a job. Not in pious rhetoric, but in reality.

Paul of Tarsus had a deliberate habit of spending anywhere from three months to three years with a church, equipping it to function in his absence. He would always then leave those churches on their own without a clergy. More on this later.

Question: Is it possible that in our efforts to bring renewal and change to the traditional church, we have never seriously taken a biblical, historical, and practical look at the legitimacy of the modern pastoral office? Can we at least experiment with another alternative...the ministry paradigm that we find in our New Testaments? For those of us who are inclined to delivering sermons and providing "leadership," do we have the integrity to freshly examine if the modern pastoral role and the giving of sermons week after week is truly equipping God's people to function as members of His Body in a coordinated way?

2. The emerging church phenomenon has neglected the role of the itinerant church planter.

Over the last few years, I have observed a number of "laymen" leave their present congregations to start new "emerging churches." Strikingly, these laymen always become the pastors of these new churches. With a few minor exceptions, the wineskin proved identical to the old wineskin that they had left.

Let me enlarge this observation into a principle. The clergy-led institutional church is like a rubber band. No matter what it experiences in the way of renewal or reform, it will always bounce back to the same structure. It lives on fads and gimmicks. But when the smoke clears, it will always return to a pastor who preaches sermons to a passive congregation, a prescribed order of worship where God's people are not free to function unhindered in the gatherings, and a building whose structural arrangement encourages people to be muted spectators.

With all of our emphasis on being faithful to incarnate the Kingdom of God in the world today, we have overlooked one important ingredient for having authentic church life that is clearly envisioned throughout the entire New Testament: The paradigm of how healthy churches were planted when the church was young, free, and pure.

I have addressed this matter in great detail in my book So You Want to Start a House Church? A. Church planters were men who have previously lived in an organic expression of church life as non-leaders before they were sent out to plant churches. One main reason: They needed to first experience that which they would pass on to others elsewhere.

B. Church planters were specially equipped to bring people into a living encounter with Jesus Christ, to teach them how to function in a church meeting, and to solve problems that the church would face in the future.

C. After the church planters had properly equipped the church to function under the Headship of Jesus Christ, they left those churches on their own without any stated leaders! (In some cases, the church planters would later return to acknowledge elders in the advent that God's people would face a personal crisis, but elders never monopolized the ministry nor took the direction away from the church.)

Question: Is it possible that the emerging church phenomenon has neglected to look at the way churches were planted in the first century, and instead, has opted to follow the path of modern missionary movements and traditional pastoral systems? For those of us who are considered "church leaders," are we confident enough in our ministries and in the ability of God's people, as well as the Holy Spirit, to abandon our congregations without stated leaders like Paul of Tarsus did...and really test the effectiveness of our ministries? Can we, pray tell, at least begin to dialogue about this matter openly and seek to discover if in fact God has rooted some unchangeable principles of church planting in His Word? Principles that may be worth returning to in our time?

3. The emerging church phenomenon has overlooked what Paul calls "the eternal purpose" (Ephesians 3:11), which is God's ultimate intention in creation and redemption.

It has been my observation that the entire thrust of the emerging church phenomenon is rooted in how best to meet people's needs. Consider the hot topics in the emerging church conversation today: "How can we better evangelize the lost?" "How can we better live out the ideals of the gospel of Jesus," "How should we treat the homosexual?" "How can we better articulate the gospel in a postmodern context?" "What is the place of artists in the church?"

All of these questions have as their underlying root the meeting of human needs. I do not mean to demean this, for the gospel certainly addresses the needs of humanity. However, there is a need in God, too. That need does not correspond to a deficiency in Himself (for He is all-sufficient), but it rather flows out of the desire of His nature. Paul calls this need "the eternal purpose" or "the purpose of the ages." And the church, as dreamt in the heart of God, stands at the heartbeat of this ultimate intention. I have read reams of emerging church articles, but never once have I seen an article (or a chapter from an emerging church book for that matter) that discusses or brings light to the eternal purpose of God.

Describing the eternal purpose of God is beyond the scope of this article, though I have addressed it elsewhere. But I wish to end this section with some searching questions:

God conceived a purpose in eternity past. And that purpose was the very motivation for the creation wherein we stand. Do you know what that purpose is?

God's eternal purpose is His magnificent obsession...it is that which drives and consumes His very being. Can the emerging church emerge from emphasizing how to better meet the needs of humanity to a conversation on that all-governing purpose which stands at the center of the beating heart of God?

4. The emerging church phenomenon shares a common trait with most of Christendom in that it is largely built on theory with little practice. For instance, there is a great deal of high-talk about Body functioning, community life, and equipping the saints for ministry, yet I have seen little to no fleshing out of these spiritual realities in any form among those who carry on loudly about them. While I applaud the gains that some emerging churches have made in providing more freedom to their members during a church service than the garden-variety institutional church, in my assessment, these churches have moved just a few inches forward on a very long road.

Allow me to enlarge this point a bit. About two months ago, I received a phone call from a well-known leader in the emerging church. His words to me were, "Frank, I'm really discouraged. There's a lot of talk about community life, Body functioning, and Body ministry among us, but I have not been impressed with what I've seen along these lines."

I agreed with him totally. But then I responded, "I believe this is a major weakness of the emerging church conversation. I certainly don't claim to have all the answers, but I've been emerging from the institutional church for almost 20 years now. I've made a lot of mistakes and failures, but I have also made many wonderful discoveries along the way. This journey continues till this day. But I can say this without flinching: For the last seventeen years, I have been gathering with Christians outside the organized church. Without exception, all of the groups that I have gathered with or have worked with personally have known the pains and joys of community life in bed-rock reality, they have all had consistent meetings under the Lord's Headship without a leader or facilitator, they have made decisions together, and they have solved their own problems . . . all without a pastor, or a group of selected men to rule them, and without a song leader or worship team."

The man never inquired further.

This leads me to a set of thorny questions: If we are humble enough to admit that a great deal of the emerging church conversation is arm-chair philosophy, can we be humble enough to sit with those who have had some practical experience in these matters and openly dialogue about them?

Is it possible for those churches that have traveled a few feet in the right direction in "liberating the laity" to not excuse themselves from examining the vast remaining tract of land to be traveled?

How will the church of Jesus Christ ever be visible on this earth in any wide measure if those whom God has called and gifted to help equip God's people are never willing learn from one another and seek to put into practice the vision that burns in their hearts? Are we each left to independently reinvent the wheel...every-man for himself? Or does this really boil down to a blatant unwillingness to abandon the clerical system which continues to control God's people? Are we blithely opting for more Band-Aids simply because it is convenient?

5. While the emerging church phenomenon has placed a much needed emphasis on the Jesus of the Gospels, it has focused on imitating His outward conduct instead of exploring His internal relationship with an indwelling God which was the source of His conduct.

Studying the earthly example of Jesus Christ and trying to imitate it is like trying to create an orange out of whole cloth by studying the composition of a natural orange in a laboratory. An orange is the fruit...the natural outcome...of the life of an orange tree. In the same way, Jesus' earthly conduct was simply the fruit of a life lived in communion with an indwelling Father.

Jesus said clearly that He could not live the Christian life: "Without my Father, I can do nothing." What, then, was the taproot of His selfless lifestyle? He gave us the answer in John 6:57, "As the Father has sent me and I LIVE BY MY FATHER, so he that eats me shall live by me." Jesus Christ had an internal relationship with His Father who indwelt Him.

For you and I to try to live the Christian life is like expecting a cat to set a dinner table, bake a cake, eat it with fork and knife, and wash dishes. The cat is the wrong life form to carry out these activities; hence, it is impossible for a cat to display human conduct. Jesus said as much when He told His followers, "Without me you can do nothing." The secret to Jesus' extraordinary life on earth was in His partaking of His indwelling Father and living by His life. In the same way, the secret to imitating Jesus is no different. It is found in partaking of our indwelling Lord and living by His life.

Can we be honest enough to admit that trying to imitate Christ's earthly life is a study in failure? Is it possible for us to take a fresh look at the Lord's earthly life by examining His internal walk as the pattern for us to imitate? For what the Father was to Jesus Christ, Jesus Christ is to you and I. Note His words: "As the Father has sent me, so I send you" (John 20:21)..."As I live by the Father, so he that eats me shall live by me." (John 6:57). It is my opinion that these words embody an entire world for Christians that has been virtually unexplored.

6. While the emerging church phenomenon has done a stellar job in emphasizing narrative in the Gospel story, it has neglected to take seriously the value of the narrative of the entire first century church as a necessary model for interpreting the New Testament.

Most of us who are part of the emerging church phenomenon take the New Testament seriously. Nevertheless, we are all handling a New Testament whose letters are out of chronological order and whose books are divided up into chapters and verses. This makes understanding the social-historical context and setting of the New Testament writings virtually impossible to grasp. And it opens the door to such spiritual hazards as isolated proof-texting to "prove" doctrines and theological systems.

Since the Protestant Reformation, we Christians have been taught to be reductionists when it comes to Bible study and individualists when it comes to applying the words of Scripture. The emerging church phenomenon has not fully shed itself from these two misguided tendencies. Consider these two thoughts which are open to challenge and dialogue:

A. The New Testament must be approached holistically if it will be understood in its right context. That is, we must step back and see the whole picture before we can properly understand the frames which make it up.

B. The Christian faith is intensely corporate. For instance, the vast bulk of the Epistles in the New Testament are written to churches...corporate bodies of believers who knew a shared life together, and not to individuals. (Out of the 21 Epistles in the New Testament, only 5 were written to individuals. And 4 of those 5 were written to Christian workers.)

Point two opens up another universe altogether that I believe must become part of the emerging church conversation. That is, living the Christian life does not work except in a shared-life, face-to-face community of believers.

When a person understands the first-century narrative, they are keen to learn that all the passages in the New Testament on transformation are not addressed to followers of Jesus as individuals. They are instead addressed to communities, a la, "churches" in the first-century sense of the word. Consequently, warming a pew and listening to sermons does not transform us. Neither does standing near a pew or chair, with hands lifted, and singing praise songs led by a worship team or music director. Transformation occurs when a community of believers discover how to behold the Lord together and live their lives in a shared way.

It seems to me that what is needed, then, is a brand new approach to the New Testament. A holistic approach wherein we understand the story...the narrative...that lies behind all of its writings. Unless we have a good grasp on how the story of Acts chronologically interacts with Paul's letters and the other letters of the New Testament, we will continue to make the common mistake of taking verses out of their historical context and misapplying them in a misguided quest for relevance.

This leads me to some terse queries. Would it be worthwhile for those of us who are "emerging" to also emerge in the way we approach the New Testament? Is it possible that grasping the narrative of the story of the early church as a background to all the Epistles can revolutionize our understanding of God's written Story and bring us further along in the church renewal/restoration effort? Is it possible that if we continue to take the individualistic, reductionist approach to the New Testament that has dominated the Christian landscape for centuries, that we will continue to make the same mistakes that our forefathers have made? Can we...and should we...utterly abandon the "cut-and-paste-stitching-verses-together-proof-texting" method of Bible study and sermonizing, and seek to embrace something better?

7. The emerging church phenomenon, like all preceding reform/renewal movements, has emphasized a bundle of Christian "its" and "things," instead of the Person of Jesus Christ.

In my opinion, if we were to examine the broad canvas of Christian movements and denominations throughout church history, we would discover that each one paints with a very fine brush. For one movement, the brush is evangelism. For another, it is social justice and acts of mercy. For another, it is praise and worship. For another, it is Bible study and doctrinal/theological accuracy. For another, it is the power of God, the gifts of the Spirit, signs and wonders. For another, it is changing the political system. For another, it is spiritual warfare and intercessory prayer. For another, it is personal prophecy. For still another, it is end-time theology (eschatology). And on and on it goes.

All of these brushes represent Christian "things." And they are just that..."things." They are Christian "its." Subjects about the Lord with which to become engaged, at best. Or with which to become obsessed, at worst.

But where are those who paint with the all-inclusive brush and talk about the Person of Jesus Christ? Where are those who are not talking about "its," "things," and "subjects" . . . but who are talking about HIM in depths little known and explored? And not just talking about Him, but who are presenting and ministering Him to His people?

Earlier I stated that I have read reams of emerging church articles. While many of them reveal fresh thinking on many subjects, I discovered something missing in virtually all of them:

I remember reading a few emerging church articles not too long ago, and I actually counted how many times the Lord was mentioned. In one article, which was quite lengthy, He was mentioned once. In another, He was never mentioned at all!

By contrast, if one were to read the letters of Paul with a careful eye, they would find his pen dripping with Christ. Take, for instance, his letter to Ephesians and Colossians. Try counting how often Paul mentions His Lord in a single chapter. It is mind-boggling!

What is my point? Paul had a living encounter with His Lord that shook him to his foundations. A ministry was born out of that encounter. And that ministry was a Person! Paul did not occupy himself with Christian "things." His occupation was the Lord Himself. And this glorious Lord embodies all things spiritual.

May I venture a searching question to my fellow ministers in the emerging church? Is it possible that we have missed the main point of our faith? Are we simply passing on the worn out tools we have been given by our evangelical forefathers on how to know the Lord? ("pray and study your Bible"..."pray more and study your Bible more!") Could there be new tools to know our Lord deeply and practically? If there are, are we open to discover them together? And are we willing to experience them before we preach them to God's people?

Do our writings and messages betray an intimate familiarity with the One who indwells us, or are we merely engaging in subjects, issues, topics, things, and its? Are our ministries one of giving LIFE...which is Christ Himself, or do we betray a vague familiarity with this glorious Person? Are we educating God's people on "subjects" about the faith, or are we bringing them into a living encounter with Him. The likes of which will consume and captivate their hearts for the rest of their lives?

In the mid-20th century, Swiss watchmakers had the corner on the world market share of watches. But that changed when one of their own countrymen came out with a revolutionary new idea: The quartz watch. He presented this idea to the Swiss manufacturers and they laughed at him. They concluded it could never work, so they refused to patent the idea. Seiko, on the other hand, took one look at the quartz watch and the rest is history.

The power of a paradigm had so influenced the Swiss watch manufacturers that they could not understand the new concept of the quartz watch. Because the quartz watch had no gears, no mainspring, and no bearings, they rejected it. Their present paradigm did not allow for the new innovation. The net effect was that they lost the leading edge on watch making and they were forced to lay off thousands of workers. It was all because the quartz watch did not fit into their world view. It did not fit within their paradigm. They did not appreciate the new way because they were blinded by the old way.

It is my strong conviction that a similar paradigm shift concerning the structure and practice of the church as well as church planting is absolutely crucial if the Body of Christ will reflect the dream in God's heart and have any significant cultural impact. Or to put it another way, a serious rethinking of the modern pastoral role, the way that churches are planted, the centrality of Jesus Christ, the taproot of Christ's earthly conduct, the narrative of the first-century story, and the eternal purpose of God are all necessary if the emerging church has any hope of fully emerging.

So consider this article as both a challenge and an invitation for patient dialogue and fellowship among leaders, authors, bloggers, and members of the emerging church community.

It would bring me great joy to have the opportunity to discuss these matters with those who have been captured with the call to emerge. For perhaps in doing so, we can learn from one another and take advantage of the present window of change that God has set before us.

www.ingramcontent.com/pod-product-compliance
Lightning Source LLC
Chambersburg PA
CBHW052037070526
44584CB00016B/2073